CHICAGO PUBLIC LIBRARY

R00862 80840

W9-AXC-326

QH
104.5
.P32
K36
1991

Kane, Karen.

America's rain
forests.

$45.00

DATE			

Clearing Branch
The Chicago Public Library
5643 W. 63rd Street
Chicago, IL 60638
767-5657

BAKER & TAYLOR BOOKS

AMERICA'S
Rain Forest

AMERICA'S
Rainforest

Gerry Ellis and Karen Kane

NorthWord
PRESS, INC
BOX 1360, MINOCQUA, WI 54548

QH
104.5
.P32
K36
1991
cop.1

*This book is dedicated to those who have worked to save
the last stands of North America's rain forest. Your dedication
and tireless efforts will be appreciated by generations to come.*

Photography Copyright © 1991 Gerry Ellis
Text Copyright © 1991 Karen Kane

All rights reserved. No part of this work
covered by the copyrights hereon may be
reproduced or used in any form or by any
means—graphic, electronic or
mechanical, including photocopying,
recording, taping or information storage
and retrieval systems—without the prior
written permission of the publisher.

Design: Bill Lundborg
        Minneapolis, MN

Printed in Singapore.

NorthWord Press, Inc.
Box 1360
Minocqua, WI 54548

For a Free Catalog describing
NorthWord's line of nature books and
gifts, call 1-800-336-5666.

Library of Congress Cataloging-in-Publication Data

Kane, Karen.
    America's rain forests / by Karen Kane; photographs by Gerry Ellis.
  — 1st ed.
        p.   cm.
    ISBN 1-55971-129-9 : $45.00
      1. Rain forest ecology — Northwest Coast of North America.
    2. Rain forests — Northwest Coast of North America. 3. Forest
    ecology — Northwest Coast of North America. 4. Old growth
    forests — Northwest Coast of North America.   I. Title.
      QH104.5.P32K36   1991
      508.315'2'09795 — dc20   91-700
                                                            CIP

CONTENTS

FOREWORD

The magnificent images and lucid text contained in *America's RainForest* demonstrate one truth with great clarity: the ancient forests of Douglas fir, western red cedar, Sitka spruce, hemlock and other tree species which cloak the land from southeast Alaska through British Columbia, Washington and Oregon to northwestern California comprise one of the most beautiful, diverse, fragile and important ecosystems in the world. The people of the United States and Canada rightfully treasure them as an incomparable legacy. On the other hand, the official governmental policies of both nations have put these forests in the way of systematic annihilation.

We hear a lot these days about the imperilled rain forests of Central and South America and other parts of the tropical world — and we should. Aside from what they contribute to the world in biological diversity, these tropical forests contribute a significant portion of the earth's oxygen. Humankind cannot afford to lose them without putting its own life on the planet in jeopardy.

But the less-publicized ancient forests of Canada and the United States have their own measure of value and it, too, is immense. The trees alone are an extraordinary resource; some of the Douglas fir, for example, are among the oldest living things on earth, dating back as much as a thousand years. But trees alone do not make a true ancient forest, which is a richly complex tapestry of interdependent plant and animal species. There is nothing quite like this web of species. From the birds that live in their canopies to the bacteria that live in their soils, from flowers to fishes, the sheer weight of living matter in the ancient forests is larger than that in any ecosystem anywhere. Their value as a biological resource is incalculable not only to the ecological health of the natural world but to human health as well. In recent years, for example, the importance of the wild Pacific yew, endemic to many of these ancient forests, was demonstrated in curing some types of cancer. No one knows how much more scientific or medical value these forests contain. We do know that the value of what they give us in recreational and spiritual enhancement is unsurpassed.

A great treasure indeed. But since the nineteenth-century era of the timber barons, these forests have been treated with careless abandon. Logged out, roaded over, mutilated and exposed to the inexorable forces of erosion, human intervention caused soil depletion, river sedimentation and wholesale disappearance of natural habitat. Detailed, scholarly studies by the Wilderness Society have concluded that no more than 10 percent of the original ancient forests of the Pacific

Northwest remains. If current levels of logging approved (and indeed promoted) by the U.S. Forest Service and the Bureau of Land Management are allowed to continue, within ten to fifteen years all we will have left for the future will be a handful of small, isolated tracts of arboreal zoos.

The forests deserve better from their human stewards. Over the past several years, the Wilderness Society has invested expertise, time and money in a concerted effort to bring these forests out of the shadow of extinction. In 1990, our ecological studies went a long way toward persuading the U. S. Fish and Wildlife Service to place the northern spotted owl, a leading resident of ancient forests in the lower forty-eight states, on the list of threatened species under the aegis of the Endangered Species Act. Our highly sophisticated map studies virtually forced the Forest Service to revise its overoptimistic estimates of remaining old growth forests. The Society's contributions were similarly important in bringing the Forest Service to establish Habitat Conservation Areas in which at least some ancient forests would be protected, simultaneously protecting the spotted owl.

None of this was, or is, enough. In spite of being revised downward, Forest Service estimates of remaining ancient forests remain grossly out of line with reality, and the levels of timber harvesting it continues to approve are much too high. The Habitat Conservation Areas it has established to protect the spotted owl may be good enough for the owl (although that, too, is highly questionable) but they do not include the amount of ancient forest they should. On its own lands, the Bureau of Land Management continues to cut as if nothing at all had transpired since it first took over responsibility for several million acres in southwestern Oregon after World War II.

Much remains to be done. The Wilderness Society is taking another hard look at forest management in southeast Alaska and is working aggressively toward legislation to assure the future of the ancient forests. The conservation community will stay in this fight. We see no other choice if the last of these splendid, imperilled forests are to be saved from blind expedience. In the meantime, for a spectacular introduction to precisely what is at stake, turn the page.

Gaylord Nelson
Counselor, The Wilderness Society

This is the forest primeval. The murmuring pines and the hemlocks,
Bearded with moss, and in garments green, indistinct in the twilight,
Stand like Druids of eld, with voices sad and prophetic,
Stand like harpers hoar, with beards that rest on their bosoms.

Henry Wadsworth Longfellow

SURVIVORS OF TIME

Carpeting the western edge of North America is a forest of magnificent proportions. It rivals any forest on earth in size and splendor. Cool, wet and forever green, it shelters an abundance of life, including some of the earth's oldest and largest living things. Perpetual currents of mild, humid air caress the coastline. Miles inland, gentle rains saturate the shaggy limbs of ancient trees on mountain slopes. At their feet, fungi harvest the stored sunlight of a dozen centuries. And in the wake of a fallen giant, seedlings crowd to gather the precious light. Thousands of years have passed this way in America's rain forest.

In the fall of 1805, Meriwether Lewis and William Clark led a small party of explorers down the vast open waters of the lower Columbia River. Over the millennia, the waters had cut a magnificent gorge through an impressive range of mountains. As the party journeyed westward, the arid sage and steppe land changed to a lush green forest. Undulating hillsides were obscured beneath a dense carpet of evergreen trees. Western hemlocks, Douglas fir, western redcedar and Sitka spruce of heights beyond their imagination dominated the landscape. The explorers had discovered an ancient temperate rain forest, the likes of which is unequaled on earth. For the remainder of their journey, the land was covered with unbroken forest to the edge of the continent.

Remnants of a lost era, conifers festooned with graceful cones reigned supreme in this forest edging the sea. They dominated the landscape for over two thousand miles in a thin green margin between the waves of the Pacific and the snow-capped peaks of mountain ranges. But this ancient ecosystem, nurturing the richest diversity of coniferous trees in the world, has been severely diminished since Lewis and Clark explored this natural masterpiece.

The Pacific forest blanketed seventy thousand square miles. The land was rich and fertile. Animals roamed freely, salmon filled the rivers and bands of Native Americans lived in balance with the ways of the ancient forest. Today, only remnants of the original forest exist. Since the mid-1800s, the ancient trees have been harvested by lumber barons and others who exploited the riches of the West. The forest seemed infinite. Cutting was intense, and replanting was unheard of until the middle of the next century. By then, it was too late.

The greatest, most productive forest on the continent was reduced to fragmented islands scarcely large enough to sustain the biotic communities contained within them. Since World War II, the few remaining tracts not protected in parks or wilderness areas have been further diminished with little thought to the effects on other species.

The western reaches of northern California, Oregon, Washington, British Columbia and southeast Alaska contain only small pockets of an ecosystem that flourished for millennia. Each harbors numerous species exclusive to their locale which evolved over eons of time. What took nature thousands of years to create

◄
Abundant precipitation gives rise to the most spectacular temperate rain forest in the world. In classic wild-river form seen from Alaska to California, the White Chuck River in the Mt. Baker/ Snoqualmie National Forest carves its way through the dense maze of ancient conifers and deciduous undergrowth. — White Chuck River, Mt. Baker/ Snoqualmie National Forest, Washington

Chapter title page — Epiphyte-covered big leaf maple — *Hoh River Valley, Olympic National Park, Washington*

11

▲
The coastal ranges form a
barrier to eastward-
moving, moist weather.
Spectacular ancient for-
ests also exist on the
eastern side of the moun-
tain ranges. Although not
as large, trees of eastern
forests, including pon-
derosa and lodgepole
pines, attain great size
and age. — *Queen Char-
lotte Islands, B.C.*

◄
Along the remote
stretches of British Columbia and Alaska,
undisturbed temperate
rain forest borders to the
Pacific Ocean's edge. Gla-
ciation, wind and surf
have created the rarest
and most spectacular wil-
derness on earth. —
*Behm Canal, Misty Fiords
National Monument, Alaska*

has been undone in less than one century.

Like the tropical rain forest, the temperate rain forest is a priceless resource,
the benefits of which extend to the entire
world. Both support a great diversity of
life, on which humans are unquestiona-
bly dependent. They store more carbon
than any other ecosystem, sustain some
of the world's most productive fisheries,
store vast amounts of water, hold keys to
treating human illness, and provide
exceptionally good building materials.

Unfortunately, ancient forests are
being replaced by tree plantations with
slight diversity. To the detriment of people, plant species and animals, their
multifold utility has been replaced by a
single commodity — timber.

More than 85 percent of the original
forest is gone, and not all of the land is
replanted.

The landscape is permanently
scarred in areas too unstable to support
new growth. The areas yet untouched
hold remnants of four distinct regions

◄
Giant trees dominate only
sections of the Pacific forest. Over 10 percent of
Alaska's Tongass National
Forest is covered in a
soggy mat called *muskeg*.
Only one tree species
grows directly in the muskeg — shore pines. They
are stunted by their
extreme environment of
abundant rain and short,
cool summers. Despite
their diminutive stature —
five to fifteen feet tall on
average — trees growing
in the muskeg may be 300
to 400 years old. —
*Revillagigedo Island,
Alaska*

which made up the greater Pacific forest: coastal rain forests, redwood forests, Douglas fir forests, and the Klamath forest. Temperature, moisture, soil conditions, age and adaptations shape and define the types of plants and animals they support.

COASTAL RAIN FORESTS The outer edge of the Pacific forest is continually saturated by winter rain and summer fog. Only fifteen miles wide, this is where the true rain forest lies. Like its tropical counterpart, this emerald string is inundated with rain — as much as two hundred inches per year.

Coastal rain forests accommodate trees which flourish in damp conditions. Because they have not been severely damaged by fire, older trees of varying ages and size flourish. Sitka spruce, western hemlock, western red cedar and big leaf maple thrive on the fog-shrouded coast and along the banks of coastal rivers.

Oregon's central coast, Washington's Olympic Peninsula, British Columbia's shattered edge and southeast Alaska's Tongass National Forest all contain small fragments of North America's rain forest.

REDWOOD FORESTS The southern tip of the Pacific forest holds the world's tallest trees — the coast redwoods of northern California and southern Oregon. They hug the coastline, growing in a 450-mile strip, on average only fifteen miles wide. Coast redwoods require tremendous amounts of ambient moisture. They thrive in the high humidity, mild temperatures and constant fog produced by the sea. Restricted to elevations below three thousand feet, they reach their zenith along stream beds brimming with an annual supply of rainfall and snowmelt, which carry fertile soil to be deposited around their thick trunks.

Coast redwoods are the tallest and oldest trees in the Pacific forest, rivaled only in age by bristlecone pines and in mass by giant sequoias. The impressive

◄

Big leaf maples are abundant in the coastal rain forest from southern British Columbia to southern Oregon. They are upholstered in a thick layer of mosses, ferns and other epiphytes. The profusion of epiphytes in the coastal rain forest is greater than in any other temperate rain forest in the world and rival that of tropical rain forests. — *Salmon River, Mt. Hood National Forest, Oregon*

◄

One of the few species of conifers capable of growing in salt mist, Sitka spruce thrive along the coastal margin of the Pacific forest. Attaining great size in a relatively short period of time, they rarely occur more than fifteen miles inland but will grow along moist, wet-stream corridors up to 100 miles from the ocean. Sitka spruce cover nearly all the forested areas of the southeast Alaskan islands which make up the Tongass National Forest. — *Pacific Rim National Park, Vancouver Island, B.C.*

redwood forest contains a greater mass of matter than any other forest in the world, including the tropical rain forest.

Redwoods retain a capacity to grow ever upwards. Often exceeding 300 feet, their stately, russet trunks taper into the sunlight, sway gently, and create a vertical landscape which confounds the senses.

DOUGLAS FIR FORESTS The Douglas fir forest of Oregon and Washington is an expanse covering the west side of the Cascade Range. It is soaked with 50 to 60 inches of rain each year. It seems a paradox that in a forest shaped by water, fire defines the region. But in autumn, wildfires race through the forest, frequently devastating large stands and altering others with less intensity.

Douglas fir seedlings thrive in burned areas because of their need to regenerate in an exposed-mineral soil. The floor of a natural forest is covered with a deep layer of slowly decaying matter which prevents the seedlings from germinating. Douglas fir are adept at regenerating in open spaces cleared of detritus. Their intolerance to shade and their need to germinate in exposed soil limits their growth in wetter, more mature coastal forests.

KLAMATH FOREST In contrast to the nearly-pure stands in the Douglas fir region, the Klamath Mountains seem wild and arbitrary. This forest shelters the greatest diversity and highest number of native species in the greater Pacific forest. The Klamaths are part of a grouping of mountains spilling over either side of the border between Oregon and California. Running east to west, they connect the Cascade and Coast ranges, an unusual feature in the Pacific region.

Throughout 40 million years, a diverse collection of species evolved in the ancient Klamath region. The Klamaths were once isolated from the rest of the continent as islands in the Pacific. The uplifting of the North American plate, which created the Cascades and the Sierra Nevadas, connected the mountains and formed a land bridge which allowed a multitude of species to migrate.

The mild climate in the Klamaths supports the growth of both coniferous and broadleaf evergreen trees. In this jumbled growth, species exist which are found nowhere else. It is a melting pot of old, rare and endangered species, which cover the full spectrum of plant life that once flourished across the continent.

Though not as biologically diverse, the Pacific forest sustains a greater mass of matter than its tropical counterpart. The temperate and tropical rain forests of the world host a preponderance of life which mankind may never fully understand. Myriad life forms are sustained by timeless biological relationships. The smallest fungi and the largest trees exist in perfect rhythm, supporting each other and a wealth of life in between.

While thousands of species of plants and animals combine to form this immensely complex ecosystem, the coniferous evergreens are the dominant force in this forest. From California's Bay Area to Alaska's panhandle, the world's largest trees have been growing in silent grandeur for almost 4,000 years.

Two hundred million years ago, conifers were the dominant form of plant life on the earth. Over time, the more adaptable flowering trees evolved, forming mixed forests. During the last 100 million years (the Pleistocene epoch) four to six ice ages ebbed and flowed. They pushed the forests south, where they were isolated in diminishing pockets or were driven into extinction.

The forests of Europe were nearly destroyed by these catastrophic events. The east-west orientation of the mountains on that continent prevented the forests from escaping the ice. But the north-south sweep of mountains on North America's west coast did not block her forests in their flight for life.

A host of climatic and geologic

changes caused the loss many of the earth's tree species, but the Pacific forest, a dinosaur of the plant kingdom, continued to exist in its primitive ways, changing little, evolving slowly. It remains a relic of the past.

The forests that harbor these mammoth trees are the most recent manifestation of similar coniferous forests that existed millions of years ago. While the plant community was different, these

► The coast redwoods are the tallest trees in the world — the tallest known approaches 370 feet. The range of the original coast redwoods has been severely diminished. Conservationists began working to save groves of coast redwoods in the mid-1800s but were largely unsuccessful. Beginning again with renewed commitment in 1918, conservationists fought for nearly fifty years to get a mere 106,000 acres protected in the Redwood National Park. — *Lady Bird Johnson Grove, Redwood National Park, California*

ancient forests contained the ancestors of species found in the forests today.

The present forests have not been drastically disturbed since the last ice sheets retreated north, about 12,000 years ago. For thousands of years their pristine quality was changed only by the sculpting hand of nature. Fire, drought, disease and wind storms never drastically altered their basic design, although these natural disturbances defined their evolution.

In the beginning, pine trees covered the region. Giving way to Douglas fir, then hemlock, and finally to the venerable cedar, the coniferous forests grew and matured. What they will evolve into

► Redwoods are the largest trees in the Pacific forest, but they produce the smallest cones.

▲
Douglas firs dominate the landscape on the western slope of the Cascade Range in Oregon and Washington. They grow throughout the West but reach their greatest size in the Pacific forest. Douglas firs are the most important timber trees in North America. For this reason, the ancient stands are being severely depleted. A major cash crop, ancient Douglas firs command top prices from Japanese and Korean markets. Douglas firs grow quickly in their first sixty to seventy years, but then their growth slows and the wood develops its tight, straight-grained, knot-free qualities. — *Above the Lewis River, Washington*

◄
A tiny hemlock seedling begins life on the trunk of a Douglas fir. Hemlocks, unlike the host Douglas firs on which they often germinate, are able to sprout and grow in the dense understory created by the ancient forest. — *Gifford Pinchot National Forest, Washington*

▲
Western hemlocks, if left undisturbed, will eventually replace other coniferous trees in a stand, creating a climax, or self-perpetuating, forest. This rarely occurs, however, as the Pacific forest is often subject to devastating disturbances such as fire, wind storms and, most destructive, logging. — *Umpqua National Forest, Washington*

centuries. Now, the epic forests of the Middle East no longer exist and their destruction forever changed the face of the planet.

Tasmania, New Zealand, southern Chile, northern Asia and Europe once harbored expansive temperate rain forests. Most of them have fallen to human need or greed. The temperate forests of the Middle East, where civilization began, were the first to disappear from the earth; the temperate forests of North America may well be the last. The legendary forest of Mesopotamia serves as a warning for the Pacific forest. A reminder that what seems an endless resource is in reality a fragile masterpiece, never to be reproduced in its original form.

Surviving on the outer edge of the continent, the Pacific forest covers the steep slopes, high mountains and the outermost islands. With remarkable tenacity, the forest takes hold on almost every type of terrain, and grows in every type of soil, however poor. An incredibly rich environment, yet it survives ironically in the poorest conditions. It lives off of itself; conserves all, utilizes everything, wastes nothing.

The landscape is astonishing. Forests border to the sea, rise from high desert plains and are swallowed by deep ravines fed by pure waters from melting glaciers. Nearly every inch of the region harbors luxuriant growth. As consistent as it appears, it is a varied and complex ecosystem. From arid eastern mountains to western rain-drenched slopes, the forest is a collection of diverse species created by a unique set of conditions.

Coastal weather patterns play a significant role in conifers' ability to thrive in the Pacific region. While hardwood or mixed forests surpassed the conifers in other temperate regions of the world, the long wet winters and hot, dry summers of the Pacific coast were adverse to their cyclical needs. No other area on earth has the weather conditions necessary to cre-

next is uncertain. Given protection, they will be forever in a state of transition.

Other forests have not been so fortunate. Forests once cloaked vast expanses of the earth. A tremendous fir and cedar forest covered ancient Mesopotamia, an area now surrounded by endless desert. The ancestors of those who now live from Greece to Egypt to Yemen lived in communities that thrived on timber. The cedars of Lebanon, made famous by the cities and temples that served King Solomon and other ancient rulers, now take their place next to past civilizations in ancient history. A growing economy and burgeoning population forced the demise of those forests in just a few short

▲
Though not as biologically diverse as tropical rain forests, the Pacific rain forest supports the greatest amount of biomass of any forest in the world. Much of this is contained in fallen trees and other woody debris. — *Siuslaw National Forest, Oregon*

◄
Because of the climate and weather, conifers dominate the Pacific forest, except in mild microclimates. The Klamath forest is the region's oldest area and contains the highest diversity of plant species. Stands of rare conifers, including Port Orford cedar, sugar pine and incense cedar, grow amid broadleaf trees such as tanoak, madronne and golden chinquapin. — *Siskiyou National Forest, Oregon*

▲
Multnomah Falls plummets 620 feet from densely-forested slopes into the Columbia Gorge. Spectacular waterfalls like this gave rise to the name of the Cascade Range. — *Columbia River Gorge National Scenic Area, Oregon*

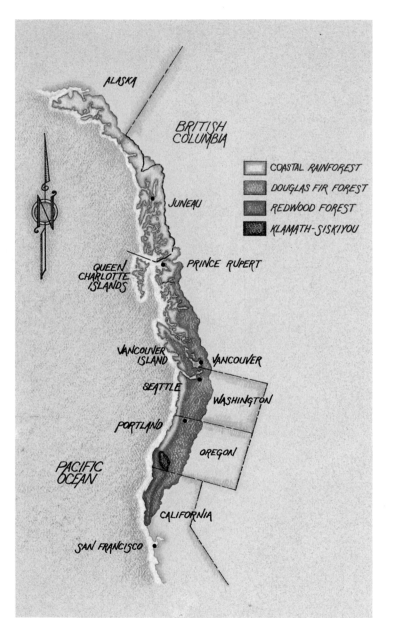

ALASKA

BRITISH COLUMBIA

N

JUNEAU

□ COASTAL *RAINFOREST*
▨ *DOUGLAS FIR FOREST*
▨ *REDWOOD FOREST*
■ *KLAMATH-SISKIYOU*

QUEEN CHARLOTTE ISLANDS

PRINCE RUPERT

VANCOUVER ISLAND

VANCOUVER

SEATTLE

WASHINGTON

PORTLAND

OREGON

PACIFIC OCEAN

CALIFORNIA

SAN FRANCISCO

ate and maintain a forest of such magnificence.

Although conditions vary slightly within the Pacific forest, a number of intermingling components help make this area one of unique biological diversity. Over the Pacific Ocean, a seasonal shuffle between high and low pressure systems fuels the extremes in weather common in much of the range. In summer, a high pressure system between Hawaii and the west coast of North America spins clockwise, blocking a northern low pressure system and allowing clear weather to be sent to the west coast. In winter, the system moves south, permitting the low pressure system to send storms from the Gulf of Alaska down to collide with the west coast.

The drenching storms which pummel the coast are attributed to the Kuroshio, an ocean current that originates near Japan, and sweeps unabated eastward across the north Pacific Ocean. The warm water of the Kuroshio supplies the air with heat and moisture, and moderates the temperature on the strip of land west of the Cascades. Coalescing droplets form storm fronts that can stretch hundreds of miles north to south, climb over 30,000 feet into the atmosphere and rain down upon the North American coastline for days on end.

On meeting the continent, clouds roll into the coastal ranges. The mountainous islands of southeast Alaska, the Coast Mountains of British Columbia, the Olympic Mountains of Washington and the Coast Ranges of Oregon and California (including the Klamath and Siskiyou Mountains) form an unbroken chain that parallels the coast. On average, the peaks reach three to eight thousand feet, but on occasion, penetrate the sky at over 10,000 feet. Snow fields and glaciers cap much of the higher altitudes, supplying a consistent reservoir of water for the forests of the Pacific slope.

This balance of uplift and rock born

◀
The Pacific forest, stretching 2,000 miles along the coast of North America, consists of a variety of evergreen trees. Over millennia weather and geology have defined four general ecological zones where certain species dominate, but these species do occur in adjacent areas where topography has created sub-climates. Additionally, within valleys and atop ridges, climate may vary significantly enough to allow non-typical species to survive. Nowhere is this more dramatically displayed than in the Klamath region, the most biologically diverse region in western North America. Today, most of the original forest has been reduced to tiny patches, which if illustrated, would appear as nothing more than specks on the map. This map simply shows the range of possible growth, not the actual blanketing of any forest type.

▶
The Pacific rain forest evolved in the most spectacular landscape on earth. Sculpted by ice, sea and wind, coastal margins of rock and ice continue to form barriers to forest migration. — *Misty Fiords National Monument, Alaska*

▲
Clouds pushed by winds
collect in openings cre-
ated by the multi-layered
canopy of the ancient
forest.

of volcanos also forms a substantial barrier to moisture-laden clouds on the journey eastward. Nearly all of the ocean
generated moisture will fall on the western slope of the mountain ranges. As
clouds rise along the coastal face of the
mountains, they loose their warmth and
drop their precious payload of rain on
the slopes below.

For up to six months in the darkest
and coolest part of the year, the west-
facing forests are bathed in life-giving
water. Warm, moist winds nourish the
land. Thin sheets of rain continually
sweep eastward. Rainbow-hued mist
drifts through the canopy, river valleys,
ridges, and hillsides cloaked in green
luxuriance.

Rain is less prevalent in the summer
months, although the coastal mountains
continue to be saturated by thick fog
coaxed in by warm air massed in the
inland valleys. Rain is the foundation for
the perpetuation of the Pacific forest.

Throughout the year, these weather
systems control the unusual seasonal
extremes. Because of this unusual
weather pattern, conifer trees abound
and deciduous broadleaf trees are sparse
and are limited to a few milder microclimates within the range. Broadleaf trees
need moisture in the warmer months —
the time of year when they are able to use
the sun's light to grow. In much of the
Pacific forest, however, summers are
exceptionally dry.

The sturdy conifers have adapted to
withstand summer drought. Their ample
number of needle-like leaves have less
area exposed to the hot sun than those of
broadleaf trees. And the symbiotic relationship between the trees and underground fungi that wrap themselves
around their fine roots helps them
endure.

Among other services, the fungi help
conifers absorb water in the summer
months, while the trees provide the fungi

◄

Horsetails are a relic of some of the oldest plants on earth, dating back 345 million years. Then, ferns, clubmosses and horsetails grew to heights of 100 feet or more. Horsetails are the ancestors of present-day conifer trees.

with sugars which they cannot produce because of their inability to photosynthesize. Conifers have an added advantage because they can photosynthesize all year long, even in winter when light levels and temperatures are low. During these months, broadleaf trees loose their leaves, preventing them from photosynthesizing.

The Pacific forest is America's last great forest. At one time, up to half of the continent was forested. The Northeast was covered with a grand mixture of broadleaf and coniferous forest. Great birch forests appeared when the glaciers retreated north. Hemlock, spruce and fir trees eventually sprouted amid hardwoods such as hickory, ash, maple, birch and oak. Massive cypress and oak trees grew in the Southeast. The farmlands of the Midwest were once cloaked in an unbroken expanse of greenery.

◀

Waters originating in high alpine lakes and from glacial melt filter through dense rain forest in the central Cascade mountains. The crystalline waters emerge after percolating through a network of fine roots and rich humus to supply the headwaters of some of the most productive salmon and trout rivers in the world. — *Lake 22 Research Area, Washington*

Remnants of these virgin forests exist in tiny isolated pockets, but none are as large as the great Pacific forest. Civilization's march across the continent, ravaging the forests as it expanded, ended at the Pacific Ocean.

A meager 15 percent of the original virgin forest remains. The balance was cut to feed our timber-hungry population.

But a forest is more than trees. It is a complex association of organisms living in harmony. From lowly underground fungi to majestic orca whales, the ancient forests of the West support a multitude of life forms whose connections we've only recently begun to understand.

America's RainForest examines the forests, the trees, the plants, the animals — and the people who rely on them for their very existence. It is a celebration of their lives, and a call for their protection.

▲

The cool, moist climate of America's rain forest favors the prolific growth of at least a dozen species of ground and epiphytic ferns. The concentric spiral, or fiddlehead, of the deer fern is a common springtime sight in the forest understory. Ferns, graceful and living proof of the age and tenacity of the earth's oldest remaining plant species, flourish in the Pacific forest.

▶

Temperate rain forests are the rarest in the world. One of the few areas harboring temperate forest, Tasmania contains giant ferns and conifer trees which have been evolving for 100 million years. Like the ancient North American temperate rain forest, the land is being mercilessly pummelled for its King Billy and Huon pines, most of which are used for paper pulp or merely cut so loggers can get to the even more valuable eucalyptus. — *Weld River, Tasmania*

Continually draped in mist, the Pacific forest is made up of conifers, which have the ability to photosynthesize when both temperatures and light levels are low. — *Above the Lewis River, Washington*

▼

27

THE FOREST AND THE TREES

The ancient forest is a place of wonder and beauty. Its cathedral-like sanctuary is a place of contemplation. Filled with birdsong, the forest creates a gentle symphony. Living monuments sway gently and sing in unison as the wind sweeps through enormous branches. Growing in peaceful serenity, the ancient forest radiates an overwhelming sense of history and grandeur.

Existing on a landscape which has undergone a multitude of geological changes, the forest exudes a sense of strength and permanence. Ice-carved valleys fall from mountains which emerged from the ocean floor. Translucent streams send water pouring over algae-covered rocks. Remnants of the most recent ice age, glaciers still cover the uppermost reaches. Lashed by a fierce succession of storms, the fractured coastline is cloaked in moisture-loving vegetation. Inland, arid, rocky hillsides are held in place by communities of plants which cannot exist on the other side of the mountain.

The forest is an intricate web of trees and shrubs, plants and animals, insects and fungi. An amazing array of life perpetuates the forest and yet depends upon it for survival. Forests are among the richest natural environments on earth. The variety of life flourishing within them is astounding — life is everywhere. The underside of a leaf, deeply corrugated bark, stout branches in the upper canopy, tunnels in a decaying log — every place creates special niches for another living thing.

The forest is more than trees. It is a self-contained system where a diverse collection of plants, animals and micro-organisms have adapted over thousands of years to a physical setting created by natural processes. Each part of the elaborate system is tightly interwoven, and each contribute to the stability and existence of the whole. We are just beginning to understand how and why so many forms of life exist together, but we do know that their interrelatedness is paramount to their survival.

Adding to the complexity of biological diversity is something far more mysterious — genetic diversity. Each tree and bird and fish is not a clone of its neighbor. Rather, each individual of a species carries a specific set of genes which provides a unique character. Genetic coding dictates characteristics such as size, color and strength, and allows organisms to make necessary adaptations within their biological and physical communities. Soil conditions, location, availability of moisture and sunlight, and resistance to

◄ Shrouded in thick mist, towering hemlocks create a natural cathedral. Ancient forests often evoke overwhelming emotional responses because of their size, age and grandeur. — *Mt. Baker/ Snoqualmie National Forest, Washington*

Chapter title page — Ancient Douglas fir forest— *Olympic National Park, Washington*

Life takes hold in every layer of the forest. In the damp understory, competition for sunlight and space is intense. Spring shoots and buds vie for the little available light. — *Pacific Rim National Park, Vancouver Island, B.C.* **▼**

Trees of the Pacific forest cling to life in a variety of conditions, often incredibly adverse. — *Above the Clackamas River, Mt. Hood National Forest, Oregon*

disease and other calamities are all factors which affect individuals within a species.

Outwardly, the forest seems a gentle, simple place. But complexity fuels the ecosystem. Intact ecosystems are important not only to the species living within them, but to others who use them transitionally.

The Pacific forest supports the largest fish runs in the world. Thousands of salmon return to their forest spawning grounds after spending time in the sea. Without the clean rivers typical of a virgin forest, salmon could not successfully migrate and leave behind the seeds of the next generation.

People also depend upon forest ecosystems. Forests prevent floods and filter pollutants from the air and thus contribute to our quality of life. By-products such as food, medicine and wisely-harvested timber provide important basic necessities.

The quantity of life in the Pacific rain forest is overwhelming. Things grow everywhere: on branches two hundred feet in the air, off the side of living trees, out of rotting stumps. Large, flat limbs high above support a community of plants, birds, mammals and insects which never touch the ground. Mosses and lichens drape limbs and create a soft, spongy carpet. A patch of growth springs from the top of a fallen log, as each plant competes to absorb the sunlight.

Though it does not support as many plant and animal species as tropical rain forests, biodiversity within the Pacific region is high — particularly in the coastal and low-elevation forests, where the climate is cooler, wetter and generally more stable than the inland forests. Both temperate and tropical rain forests share warm and moist characteristics, and the absence of extreme temperature changes from season to season. However, the tropics receive a consistent supply of sunlight throughout the year; in the Pacific forest, light is in short supply for half the

▼
Struggling for a competi-
tive edge, young plants
take advantage of elevated
positions on fire-scarred
and otherwise damaged
snags. — *Lake 22
Research Area, Washington*

▲
Giant burls punctuate the
hulks of rain forest con-
ifers, often attaining
diameters twice that of
their hosts. Burl surfaces
collect fallen organic
material and serve as
nurseries for countless
young plants. —
*Carmanah Valley, Van-
couver Island, B.C*

▶

Shelf fungus begins life in the heartwood of dead trees, extending its woody, fruiting body outward and growing larger as it consumes the wood.

year.

The roles warmth, moisture and sunlight play in species diversity aren't clear. But speculation reasons that with consistent conditions and without being limited by extreme temperatures produced by changing seasons, organisms can focus their energy on refining their roles within their environment. Species are forever competing, diversifying and filling smaller and more defined ecological niches. Removed from their niche, they perish. Many of these species cannot exist outside their particular forest environments.

The temperate, coniferous forest of western North America has a variety of names: old growth, primeval, cathedral, virgin, ancient. One thing is certain: It is a true forest, a living museum which existed well before humans walked its sodden floor and cut into its heart. Much of the original forest has been destroyed, and little remains in pristine condition. The remnants are a minute legacy of a graceful giant that once covered seventy thousand square miles.

A patchwork of forests make up the larger Pacific region, and each patch is the result of its individual geologic history and microclimate. Forests of the west share common characteristics: they are all ancient, clinging to landscapes untouched by catastrophic changes for anywhere from twelve thousand to forty million years. They maintain a perfect balance of life and death; living and dying occurs simultaneously. And their structural diversity is tantamount to the species diversity found within.

The major components of old-growth forests are large, live trees (which range in age from two hundred to thousands of years); fallen trees and other woody debris in all stages of decomposition; snags (standing dead trees); and a canopy of several layers, comprised of trees of various sizes and the shrubs of the shaded understory.

LARGE, LIVE TREES Deep within the forest, towering conifers reach for precious sunlight — the basis for their existence. Each tree endures the timeless rigors of life. Majestic beings, they scatter light, provide shade, hold soil in place and guard time. Their sheer magnitude

◄
There are many similarities between temperate and tropical rain forests: a layered canopy, open understory, copious amounts of moisture and efficient nutrient cycling. Tropical forests, however, have higher diversity of life and harbor more species of flowering and deciduous plants. — *Gombe Stream Reserve, Tanzania*

Spotted owls are but one of many highly-evolved rain forest animals. Their lives are acutely adapted to the complex structure of the ancient forest.

The Pacific forest harbors the highest diversity of conifer species found anywhere in the world, along with the largest individuals of each species represented. Trees the size of this rare 600-year-old, seven-foot-diameter Douglas fir no longer cover the landscape. — *Cathedral Grove, Vancouver Island, B.C.*

▼

forces a change in perspective. Thick trunks dominate the understory. High above, a slender, weathered crown emerges from the forest cover, capturing ambient moisture and diffusing light. The straight trunks are accentuated by their nakedness — bare except for a few unevenly-spaced branches high above. Entire worlds live on these massive, flat limbs: mosses, lichens, ferns, insects, birds and small animals.

Every inch of the tree is utilized by other plants and animals. Different levels host a multitude of species, providing habitat for a dynamic congregation of life. At the tree's roots are fungi, providing essential nutrients. Bats sleep by day in deeply grooved bark. Nitrogen-fixing lichens drape across branches and attach themselves to vertical surfaces. Tiny red tree voles spend their entire lives in the upper limits of ancient trees.

FALLEN TREES The importance of live trees is equalled by the decaying wood lying randomly on the forest floor. The Pacific forest holds the highest concentration of dead wood in any forest in the world, the bulk of which is contained in large, downed trees. Logs store water for hundreds of years, control erosion, provide food and shelter for animals and

Fallen trees perpetuate the forest. Returning energy borrowed over time, they nurture new growth centuries after falling. — *Gifford Pinchot National Forest, Washington*
▼

▲
Large, live trees are one of the major components of the ancient temperate rain forest. Each tree is a collection of micro-environments — even the deeply-crevassed bark is home to insects, birds and bats.

◄
Standing dead trees, or snags, significantly increase the vertical biological and structural complexity of the ancient forest. They are a major element in the definition of ancient forests.

recycle nutrients back into the soil.

Streams also benefit from the disorderly assemblage of fallen trees. A source of energy, downed trees hold a concentration of nitrogen and other nutrients. They reduce the flow of sediments downstream, filter nearly-pure water and prevent bank erosion. In addition, the dams, plunge pools and gravel beds they create are valuable habitats for fish and other water animals.

As nutrients are derived mostly from decayed matter, the forest is fed by the massive amount of dead wood. Dead trees support the continuation of life in the forest and contribute to its rich diversity. At the time of its death, a five-hundred-year-old tree has only given half itself in its role in the environment. It continues to support life for another five hundred years.

In reality, a tree never dies. It simply converts into another form. By providing the essential components for life, dead trees assure the health of the forest by recycling borrowed energy.

STANDING DEAD TREES The strong, tall trees of the ancient forest age and eventually succumb to the rigors of weather, disease, fungi and other devastating effects. Long before it is visible, life begins to leave an ancient tree. Its top broken or trunk diseased, an ancient tree dies slowly and remains standing for decades. Snags deteriorate from top to bottom, and from outside to inside. Losing its bark, needles and branches, a three-hundred-foot monolith eventually becomes a tall stump which crumbles to the ground, continuing the cycle of death into life.

A standing dead tree is valuable to wildlife for over one hundred years. Insects, woodpeckers, birds of prey, flying squirrels, martens, bears and countless other creatures use snags for observation posts, food, nesting and shelter.

THE LAYERED CANOPY The ancient forest is a vertical mosaic, made

◄
Woody, debris-filled streams are a critical feature of the ancient forest. The debris alters water flow and forms pools and quiet waters, creating prime spawning areas for salmon and trout along with habitat for a variety of water-dependent creatures. — *Sorensen Creek, Columbia Gorge National Scenic Area, Oregon*

▶ Deciduous hardwoods such as the big leaf maple, along with red alder and vine maple dominate openings in the coniferous canopy. Spaces and corridors which remain open permanently feature moss- and lichen-festooned big leaf maples over one hundred years old. — *Salmon River Valley, Mt. Hood National Forest, Oregon*

▶ Paramount to the ancient rain forest's survival is a varied and complex mid-canopy. — *Mt. Baker/ Snoqualmie National Forest, Washington*

▲
Shade-tolerant bleeding heart.

up of trees of all ages. Viewed from above, the canopy reflects an assortment of growth. Wind damaged treetops sway above a continuous wave of cone-shaped trees. Snags pierce the canopy. Dark voids created by fallen giants dot the tree cover. In other hollows, young trees which have out-grown their neighbors emerge into the sunlight.

Greenery at different stages of growth create a tiered canopy and serve as highways for small animals and hunting grounds for aerial predators. The unbroken canopy is perfectly structured for collecting rainwater and drawing moisture from meandering fog. It is also adept at capturing ambient nitrogen which is processed by the millions of needles growing on long-lived trees.

Live trees, wood on the ground and in streams, snags, and a layered canopy are the components of an old-growth forest. Hundreds of years must pass before trees die, fall and begin to support other life. It can happen in as little as two hundred years, if left alone. Depending on the location and the landscape on which a forest must regenerate, it could take hundreds of years. It is quite possible that once destroyed, a forest may never appear in the same form. Drastically disturbed sites may never be able to support the same type of vegetation.

Over time, forests undergo physical changes. In a sequence which can last a millennium or more, forest succession takes an area from grassy undergrowth to stately trees and specialized animal species. Each stage of succession alters the area and provides a hospitable nursery for the new plants which follow.

At first, a wild assortment of flowers and shrubbery blooms in a landscape born of natural catastrophe. Carried by wind or cracked open by fire's intense heat, pioneer plants sprout in soil created by preceding generations. Shrubs spring up amid toppled trees and push their way through layers of dust and ash blown from a nearby volcano. Supplied with nutrients and water stored in dead trees, new growth flourishes in unabated sunlight. Life is unrestrained in the newly cleared area. Insects bore into fallen trees, underground fungi weave through a mother lode of dead wood and roots, while animals forage on tender new growth.

Soon, the young forest becomes a tangle of coniferous and hardwood seedlings. As the forest ages, some initial tree species die out as the conditions they require no longer exist, and other seedlings take their place. Animal communities also change. Those who benefit from open, sun-filled sites do not fare as well under the dark blanket of middle-aged forests. Those who require the secluded cover of older forests begin to move in.

The Douglas fir predominates much of the Pacific forest. Reaching skyward, Douglas firs eventually surpass all other rivals and begin to overshadow saplings and undergrowth. For hundreds of years, they rule the forest in a seral community. As older and weaker specimens die, young shade-tolerant conifers emerge from the dark forest floor. In time they dominate, replacing Douglas fir seedlings unable to grow in the dark understory.

The forest evolves into a climax community. Able to regenerate in their own shadow, climax communities can survive indefinitely if left undisturbed.

If age adds anything to the forest, it is beauty. Ancient stands of climax trees have an aura which enchants and soothes. These gigantic trees are the largest living things on earth. Though they differ within the Pacific region because of location and climate, climax forests have one thing in common — character that comes only with age.

Humid rain forests along the coast

Trees growing in the muskeg forests are stunted. Extreme environmental conditions limit their growth. — *Revillagigedo Island, Alaska*

▼

◄
Fungi are the major decomposers of downed and dying trees. Each fungus sends a fine network of root-like mycelia through the wood. It will take generations of fungi to decompose an ancient conifer.

with their mixed stands of cedar, Sitka spruce and hemlock, are carpeted with ferns, draped with lacy mosses and ribboned in lichens. Douglas fir forests take on character as a result of the hardships they face over hundreds of years. Fire scars and thick, furrowed bark attest to their resiliency. In the drier Klamath region, climax stands take on a Mediterranean look where true firs are surrounded by broadleaf evergreens, such as tan oak and madrone. In the upper reaches of the mountains where deep snow persists, Pacific silver fir and western hemlock form nearly-pure stands of tall, skinny trees able to slough off heavy snow.

As the forest ages, growth slows considerably, but its renowned integrity and rich diversity comes to fruition.

Though seemingly devoid of animals, the forest is teeming with life. More than two hundred species of animals occupy ancient forests. One hundred use it primarily, and nearly forty find only old growth suitable for nesting, breeding or foraging. As many as fifteen hundred insects live in the canopy of one tree.

On the forest floor, a black bear rips apart a rotting log in search of grubs. Elsewhere, a herd of elk forages on lichens found only in old forests. In the trees above, a Douglas squirrel scolds intruders while a pileated woodpecker drills in staccato on a snag, trying to dislodge stubborn insects. Martens and fishers scurry along the highways of branches.

In the streams, river otters snatch frogs and salamanders from nearby pools, and in the rivers, salmon return to their spawning grounds to give life to another generation.

At night, bats emerge to scour the air for insects, and spotted owls hunt silently for flying squirrels and aerial trees voles. The profusion and variety of life are constant reminders of a truly remarkable place.

Protecting and fostering myriads of

◄
Thousands of seedlings sprout in the shaded understory, but relatively few survive the rigors of rain-forest life to mature to enormous size. The advantages of beginning life on a nurse log can improve a seedling's survival chances by 90 percent.

Coastal redwoods grow to tremendous age and size — some live over 2,000 years. Individuals of this age have survived intense fire; thick bark protects their vital heartwood from flames. — *Redwood National Park, California*
▼

biological communities, the forest exhibits a resourcefulness that humans attempt but cannot emulate. The ancient forest has evolved apart from us, without help from us. Perhaps that is why it captures our imagination. Its age, strength and resiliency demands our admiration.

Designing a forest of such magnificence is beyond human ability. With age, the forest becomes self-sustaining, self-perpetuating. It requires nothing but that which is found within. The ancient forest persists by replenishing itself. In doing so, it nurtures its inhabitants with an efficiency that humans can only hope to achieve.

Thoreau wrote, "I came to the woods because I wished to live deliberately, to front only the essential facts of life, and see if I could not learn what it has to teach, and not, when I came to die, dis-

cover that I had not lived." People generally have a respect for age and for the value of what inherently belongs to the earth. Like Thoreau, we should learn the lessons of the woods before these ancient forests are gone.

▲
Snow provides a protective thermal cover for young trees in high elevations and northern latitudes.

▶
Douglas squirrels play an important role as couriers in the distribution of seeds. In fall, they travel the canopy, collecting cones and carrying them to winter caches.

Aerial Forests

Chapter title page —
Lady Fern

Perhaps no other region of the Pacific forest epitomizes the essence of rain forest as does the lush assortment of growth lying on the west side of Washington's Olympic Peninsula. Extending fifty miles into the rugged Olympic Mountains, the Hoh, Queets, Bogachiel and Quinault river valleys harbor the quintessential rain forest.

Looming trunks of some of the region's largest trees are surrounded by an exquisite cover of plant life. Gnarled stumps of three-hundred-foot giants are festooned in ferns and mosses. The forest floor is covered by a plush mat not content to limit its growth to the ground. Alders and maples line the river and are adorned with mosses and lichens which create a living mantle. Feathery draperies trail three feet from big leaf maple branches, forming archways to the inner forest.

The rain forest lining the Olympic river valleys envelops observers with solemn shades of green. Surprisingly, the inside of the forest is rather open. It is not the impenetrable jungle the term *rain forest* conveys. The understory is covered with debris, but there is no thick undergrowth. Except for having to clamber over large logs or overturned roots, walking along the Olympic rain forest's rivers is relatively easy.

There are no patches of bare ground in the Olympic river valleys. Conifer seeds germinate on fallen trees, unable to take root in soil because the competition has formed a living barrier. Everything lying on the forest floor is upholstered in soft, plush vegetation.

The imaginative names of the plants add to the enchanted ambience: haircap moss, leafy liverwort, pixie goblets. Delicate wood nymphs, fairy slippers, bleeding hearts and maidenhair ferns poke through the soft, damp sponge. The enchanting and mysterious forest understory compells the curious to investigate its witch's brew of ingredients. Chanterelles, morels, cauliflower mushrooms and hundreds of other fungi of every color in the rainbow sprout where you least expect them. Jewel lichen, Oregon lungwort and corkir climb young trees and the branches of brushy shrubs. Above, old man's beard, wolf lichen and icicle moss form graceful loops, trailing off in wispy green curtains.

The aroma of this magical concoction permeates the air. The rich scent of decomposing plant matter is pervasive in

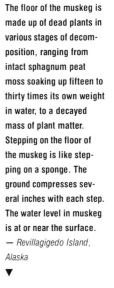

The floor of the muskeg is made up of dead plants in various stages of decomposition, ranging from intact sphagnum peat moss soaking up fifteen to thirty times its own weight in water, to a decayed mass of plant matter. Stepping on the floor of the muskeg is like stepping on a sponge. The ground compresses several inches with each step. The water level in muskeg is at or near the surface. — *Revillagigedo Island, Alaska*
▼

◄
Ferns, lichen and other plants favor big leaf maple bark. In the wettest coastal forests, these trees are draped with up to three feet of lacy moss. — *Hoh River Valley, Olympic National Park, Washington*

Fungi are an important food source for many animals. Fruiting both above and below ground, some fungi emit strong odors, attracting rodents who in turn disperse undigested spores throughout the forest.

Sword ferns, the most common and prodigious of all Pacific Coast ferns, form clumps measuring three feet in diameter. Each spring, bright green new growth sprouts from the heart. Swords are one of the few ferns which remain green throughout the year.

the moist, heavy air. Yet the fragrance is pleasant and suggests a vitality in contrast with death and decay. The constant process of death and decay on the lower level of the forest exudes fertility. Every step produces a passing whiff of life, spiced by odors from pungent plants like oyster mushrooms, skunk cabbage and vanilla leaf.

The serene forest floor is the level most familiar to the hiker. It is a soothing place. The forest understory houses an interlocking system of plants from the lowest form of lichen to flowering shrubs which intertwine with amazing complexity. Though lacking sunlight and the subsequent photosynthesis, the floor plays host to incredibly intense activity, most of which remains unseen. Bathed in splintered sunlight, life begins and ends on the forest floor.

Direct sunlight is a precious commodity. Barely reaching the forest floor, the sun is reduced to thin, slanted shafts of flickering rays that touch down momentarily. Trees, leafy shrubs and other plants which require heavy doses of sunlight languish and die. But even in this shadowy realm, the forest floor eminates wondrous beauty existing off the debris created by previous generations.

Though seldom seen, animals inhabit the forest. Even in their absence, their spirit enhances the beauty of the woodland. The ancient forest is a gentle place in which to live. Warm in winter, cool in summer, it is an idyllic setting to feed, find shelter and give birth to young.

Animals move easily through the maze of decomposing logs, finding it a warehouse of nutrition but they are discreet. Witnessing an elk, his neck stretched high, innocently nibbling bearded lichen, or a bobcat pouncing upon its ill-fated prey is a rare occurance. But they are ever-present, moving about in the hushed stillness or under the cover of darkness.

Chips of wood, a torn-apart log and gossamer veils reveal the beaver, raccoon

Although they produce thousands of tiny seeds, delicate four-inch-tall calypso orchids do not easily germinate. Instead, they rely on symbiotic relations with specific fungi to sprout and bloom.

▼

The soil underlying the thick mat of organic matter on the forest floor can be poor. Trees and plants of the Pacific forest have made remarkable adaptations to gleaning nutrients from other sources.

Each fall, the forest floor bursts into color with scores of unusually shaped fungi. Mushroom hunters prize the coral mushroom for its fine but mellow flavor.

▼

and spider. The underside of a softened log conceals tiny mice looking for truffles. A pile of sticks and twigs might be the nest of a dusky-footed woodrat. An unseen observer peering from a tunnel in a decaying log is a Pacific giant salamander. And no one knows how many species of insects crawl on, or just under, the forest floor.

As rich as the forest floor seems, the mineral soil lying underneath the lush groundcover is often poor. The Pacific region's cooler temperatures are a detriment to the decomposition of plant matter and because of this, rich forest soils form slowly. Yet plants have developed remarkable adaptations for scavenging their nutrients from the prodigious amount of dead matter lying about.

The raw alluvium deposits on the riverbanks in the Olympic forest are a good example. This sandy, loose aggregate, poor in nutrients, is colonized by plants which glean nitrogen and other elements by absorbing them from the air and assimilate them into their systems with the help of bacteria living on and within their roots.

Alders are generally the first trees to colonize open areas and often monopolize sites. Amid monotones of green, they provide a striking contrast. Looking through a pure stand, straight trunks spotted with white and dark green blotches of lichen fade off into a pink backdrop created by new growth. From a distance, the symmetry of alders' rounded tops creates a corridor of brightness and forms a border where river and forest meet.

Throughout the seasons these and other deciduous trees loose their leaves, which fall to the ground and are consumed by soil bacteria. Young shoots of shrubs become food for deer and other animals which forage along the river. The droppings the animals leave behind are converted into valuable soil nutrients by worms, insects, microscopic fungi, bacteria and protozoa. The soil is continu-

ally enriched with humus by this natural process.

As the soil continues to improve, conifers take root under the river's strip of alders and develop fine root systems which fan out into the rich upper layer of humus. Although the deepest roots of the oldest conifers generally do not extend below four or five feet, they take advantage of the alders' nitrogen-fixing bacteria. In time, the evergreens overshadow the area and the colonizers eventually die.

As conifer trees age, the team of soil decomposers continues its work, breaking down the confetti of needles, lichen, mosses and other detritus which falls continually. This rain of forest litter eventually returns nitrogen, carbon, phosphorus, hydrogen and other life-giving elements to the trees which make up one of the richest, most productive forests on earth.

The vitality of the massive trees is aided by another soil inhabitant unseen to all but the curious — or the hungry. Legions of fungi grow under the soil in which the giant trees are anchored. In symbiotic relationship, underground fungi wrap themselves around the fine roots of conifers and act as both partner and thief to the tree. These mycorrhizal associations formed by fungi and root are crucial to the health of the forest. Dispersing a web of fine threads, the fungi bond with the tree roots and assist it in assimilating valuable water and nutrients such as nitrogen. The tree repays them with sugar and amino acids which fungi cannot manufacture on their own because they cannot photosynthesize.

Amid the organic rubble on the forest floor tarries an important part in the link between the trees and the fungi. The red-backed vole resembles a furry wind-up toy racing helter-skelter out of control. The fate of the forest depends on this unlikely creature.

For the vole, life is simple and con-

Pacific tree frogs spend more time on the damp forest floor than clinging to trees, for which their long toes and toe pads have adapted. For several months each year, the frogs' musical notes pipe through the rain forest.

▲
Witches butter adds bright
color to the forest throughout the year. This jelly
fungus thrives on dead
wood.

Unlike most other con-
ifers, coast redwoods
have the ability to sprout
new growth from a fallen
tree. Small, tight circles
of giant trees mark the
spot where a parent red-
wood of a thousand years
past once stood.
▼

sists solely of procreating and eating. The vast majority of fungi which have a partnership with the roots of the conifer produce underground fruiting body. The truffle, an underground mushroom resembling a small potato, is the food on which the red-backed vole survives. In doing so, the vole unknowingly serves as matchmaker for two non-mobile partners. Because the truffle grows underground, it cannot disperse its spores on the wind. By gobbling up truffles and then venturing on in search of the next, the vole transports the tiny spores of the fungi in its stomach. Its subsequent droppings enable seedlings to form the life-giving partnership which they need in order to grow to their enormous size.

Life in the rain forest is a study in recycling. All matter has a place in life and death. Although the trees here are among the oldest living things on earth, none live forever, yct none go to waste.

After centuries of life a tree falls, destined to return the energy it has borrowed over time. The crashing giant signals a celebration of life. Tons of cellulose pound a trough two feet deep into the soft ground and cut short the lives of everything lying in its path. In its death, the fallen tree provides life in the forest. Taking as many centuries to decompose as it did to grow, a newly-fallen tree begins the languid transformation from a living entity to a humus-covered mound decaying in the rich soil it helped create.

As it decomposes into the simple elements from which it was born, a fallen tree supports thousands of other lives and serves a multitude of functions. Logs cover a quarter of the forest floor. Lying in all directions, they contribute to soil stability by forming natural terraces across slopes, thereby preventing erosion and creating soil beds on the uphill sides in which seedlings take root. The new soil beds shelter insects and small mammals including deer mice, voles and chipmunks. Lying on the perennially wet ground, the log retains moisture, which

► Skunk cabbage grows in standing water amid cedar and spruce. As its name implies, the flower has a characteristic odor, but its beauty offsets its rank smell.

► Delicate oxalis carpets the forest floor with bright green leaves and creamy white flowers in early spring, rising through autumn's fallen leaves and needles.

▲
Deer fern

◄
One of the greatest attributes of the ancient forest
is the variety of habitats it
provides. More than 180
vertebrate species thrive
and reproduce in the lush
environment. Many more,
as seemingly removed as
orca whales, are depen-
dent on the forest
ecosystem. Typically,
those creatures at the top
of the food chain suffer the
greatest negative effects
of ecosystem damage.
Bobcats, though not totally
dependent on ancient for-
ests, rely on the forest for
winter refuge, food and
habitat for raising their
young.

assists the numerous bacteria, fungi, lichens, mosses, insects, mammals, trees
and flowering plants which will eventually gather its rich wealth of nutrients.

In falling, a tree contributes to the
health of others in the forest by creating a
clear pathway to the sky. Species which
cannot survive in the dark understory
inhabit the newly-created space. Nearby
trees languishing in the dark benefit from
the sudden flood of sunlight. What was
once an area of quiet existence bursts into
rapid growth, each plant craving the light
which will again be in short supply in a
few years.

Like the forest itself, the beneficial
nature of a fallen log increases with time.
The tree's outer bark, inner bark, sap-
wood and dead, internal heartwood
eventually provide unique niches for
other forms of life. The breakdown of
wood, largely the work of minute bacteria and fungi, is initiated by insects and

carried on by voles, salamanders and
countless other animals.

The first creatures to reach the fallen
tree are beetles which make their way
through the outer bark, eager to reach
the more nutritious inner bark and sap-
wood. In doing so, they provide an entry
for other creatures hungry for the car-
bohydrates and moisture found within
the fallen warehouse.

Beetles bring along the spores of
fungi in their wastes and deposit these
major consumers of wood in the quarter-
inch tunnels they bore. Fungi fans out
into the log and because they are unable
to make their own food, they feed on the
wood. As they consume it, other organisms enter the newly-opened space, feed
on the valuable nutrients released
through rot and decomposition and further the breakdown of the log.

All the while, the moisture content of
the log increases. As reservoirs of water

▲
Lady's ferns' lacy fronds
provide a delicate contrast
to the thick, coarse bark of
giant conifer trunks. Ferns
thrive in the moist, cool
understory, occasionally
reaching three feet in
height. — *Bogachiel River
Valley, Olympic National
Park, Washington*

Bushy-tailed woodrats arrange piles of conifer sticks and cones to store food and objects as unusual as bottle caps and other human garbage.

Caterpillars and other insects are responsible for harvesting much of the annual foliage produced by rain forest hardwoods. Conifers fall victim to beetles and termites. In turn, insects supply a vital link in the forest food chain for migrating songbirds.

Red alders form pure stands along waterways. A colonizing species in disturbed sites, it holds soil and provides canopy cover for shade-tolerant conifer seedlings. Alders also prepare soil by fixing aerial nitrogen.

Sugar pine, a Sierran-forest species, extends its range into the drier, milder Klamath region. It produces the largest conifer cones in the world - eighteen inches or more. Sugar pine seeds were a favorite food among native people.

▲
Honey mushrooms are the ornate fruiting body of one of the dozens of fungi that decompose dead wood, but unlike others, this fungus also attacks live trees.

▶
The cycling of nutrients from canopy to forest floor is vital to the health of the system. Even branches of living trees harbor a wealth of plant life that will inevitably add to the richness of the soil.

Old man's beard drapes trees in the moist rain forest. A lichen, it is eaten by deer and elk and aids in absorbing nutrients from their normal food sources.

and nutrients, decomposing logs soon become nurseries for young plants and storehouses which established plants tap through the dry summer. Up to one hundred species of plants, in addition to fungi, enter a fallen log. After fungi, lichens and mosses creep from the forest floor and climb aboard, followed by herbs, shrubs and tree seedlings.

Fallen logs are ideal nurseries for seedling hemlocks and spruces. Suppliers of warmth and moisture, they provide young trees the essential elements with which to begin life. Some species of conifers unable to germinate on the moss-covered floor take hold on the surrogate log. As their roots enter the softened mass, they, too, help break down the wood, which eventually sloughs off in cube-like blocks.

Here, seedling trees are first introduced to fungi that assist them in the uptake of nutrients. Called *mycorrhizae,* this association between tree root and fungi is essential to the survival of both the tree and the non-photosynthesizing fungi. But as hospitable as a fallen log is for infant trees, it lacks an important component — mineral soil.

In their first years of growth, seedlings expend more energy sending out roots to find mineral soil than they do in forming the tree itself. A ten-year-old tree may only be one foot tall but its root system is extensive. Roots extend over the nurse log like tentacles, looking for something to grip. Once they find the necessary rich soil, the tree becomes stronger and taller, shading out thousands of competitors which sprouted in its vicinity.

In time, colonnades of enormous trees straddle slowly decomposing logs. Their serpentine roots hold the shape of their nurse log above the soft, linear mound of green compost left behind. The nurse tree, now gone, provided a function in death which lasted as long as its function in life, perhaps longer.

For some, the most visible features of

▲
Fallen trees and broken snags open the forest floor to needed sunlight. Species dependent on sunlight to germinate begin a repeated cycle on which the forest depends.

the rain forest are the most interesting: the huge trees; roots crawling over stumps and logs; vegetation growing in, on or through fallen debris; and the thick mat of moss and lichens covering every surface. The forest floor is full of life but it is death which holds this life together. By providing a base from which to sustain rich diversity, death becomes the giver of life.

▲
Ancient forest floors are a
maze of fallen trees generations deep. Each log adds
to the complexity of the
floor topography, unlike
tree plantations whose
floors are bare and vir-
tually lifeless.

▲
Competition for space on
the forest floor is intense.
Thick mats of decaying
vegetation often prevent
seedlings from germinat-
ing. Elevated on fallen
logs and stumps, their
chance for survival is
greatly improved. The
early years of a seedling's
life are spent sending long
tap roots to harvest min-
erals in the nurse log and
soil below.

▲
Hundreds of seedlings
may sprout in the first
years after a log is
downed, but only a few of
the fittest will survive to
maturity in the coming
centuries.

▲
Over hundreds of years,
the nurse log will com-
pletely decompose,
leaving in its wake a
colonnade of maturing
trees with elevated roots
and arching above a
mouldering, moss-
covered mound.

IN THE SHADOW OF GIANTS

$\mathcal{E}$arthbound, humans are privy to only a fraction of the secrets the forest conceals. Another great mystery of the rain forest is above them, beyond reach. The clear, sustained note of the varied thrush lures the curious to gaze at the treetops, but all that is visible is a two-dimensional web of limbs and needles. Glimpses of sunlight shimmer through openings created by the gently-swaying treetops. Like staring into a starry night, the familiar is still the unknown.

Out of reach, the rain forest canopy stretches beyond imagination. In the oldest forests, the great towering conifers grow to well over three hundred feet. In Vancouver Island's Carmanah Valley, a giant Sitka spruce of unparalleled size stretches into the clouds. Enormous branches emerge forty feet aloft and support entire communities. Aerial gardens of ferns, mosses, shrubs and seedling trees grow out of view from the forest floor. Along these air-bound botanical highways, martens and chipmunks travel with ease. Where the canopy has escaped destruction from the loggers saw and lies intact, a Douglas squirrel can travel endless miles without touching the ground.

As moisture-laden winds blow in from the Pacific, they embrace a rain forest canopy full of character, reflecting the years spent rooted to the earth. Incoming clouds wreath a verdant landscape of treetops mimicking the ground below. Following the contours of the land, the canopy undulates with rolling hills, climbs steep ravines and clings to

precipitous slopes. Fog droplets collected on millions of thin needles reflect the colorless sky. Snags jut through the mist-shrouded ceiling and serve as signposts. Ridgelines stacked against each other trail off into a terraced sea of green.

The symmetrical cone-shaped tops of ancient trees produce a rough texture in an otherwise somber expanse. Damaged by intense storms, fierce winds and drying sun, the canopy is in sharp contrast to the gentle atmosphere on the forest floor.

As viewed from a distance, it is difficult to comprehend that this aerial juncture of sun, water, wind, plant and animal teems with life. In the crossroads of these elements, a unique world assists the forest in maintaining its wealth of diversity. Plants and animals of this lofty haven form mutually beneficial relationships among themselves, as well as assist those who make their homes several hundred feet below. The canopy weaves an important thread into the fabric of the

◄

The ancient forest canopy is enveloped in fog and clouds for most of the year. Coastal weather patterns over the Pacific forest have remained unchanged for 7,000 years or more. — *Gifford Pinchot National Forest, Washington*

▲

Rain forest canopies are especially adept at capturing moisture from passing clouds and fog. In addition, millions of needles collect airborne dust particles and transform them into useful nutrients.

forest as a collector of water and sun, a producer of nitrogen-rich plants and a major contributor to the floor's supply of nutritious debris.

Reaching to touch the sun, trees collect solar energy. Much of the forest's growth takes place in the canopy because of the sun's intensity. The towering trees are limbless except near the top. A layering of heavy, fan-shaped branches support needles which provide nutrients for the trunks and roots living on the shadowy floor. Conifer branches form tall, thin, angular crowns. Unable to capture sunlight and passing fog, the branches are naturally pruned. Chunky cones full

◄
Needles and other organic debris raining down from the forest canopy feeds plants, mosses, lichens and fungi on the forest floor. British soldiers, a lichen, is a combination of fungi and algae growing together in a symbiotic relationship. The stalk and bright red cap of this lichen is its fruiting body.

◄
Standing dead trees help increase the structural and biological diversity of the ancient forest and create a wide variety of habitats.
— *Siskiyou National Forest, Oregon*

of seeds form far above the forest floor.

All life in the forest depends on the collection of branches and needles crisscrossing the sky above where photosynthesis is concentrated. Millions of needles glean light from even the grayest skies, capturing the energy from the sun and using it to convert water, carbon dioxide and minerals into oxygen and other energy-rich organic compounds. Transformed into wood and foliage, the sun's energy produces food for animals and other plants.

Consisting of trees of all sizes and ages, the canopy of the ancient rain forest is broken and uneven. Fog rolling in from the coast envelops the canopy in a cold, moist blanket. The tree crowns are adept at wringing moisture from this fog and from passing clouds.

An ancient tree can support more than sixty million needles. The surface area of these thin leaves covers forty thousand square feet. Fog drip from needles accounts for 25 percent of the moisture supply in some areas. This ability to harvest water from the sky is critical during the summer months when rainfall is low and evaporation is high.

◄
Coast redwoods thrive in a thin, fog-prone belt along the northern California coast. — *Redwood National Park, California*

◄
Stout conifer branches become aerial gardens of ferns, mosses, lichens, trees and shrubs. In the ancient rain forest, life takes hold virtually everywhere.

Viewed from above, the canopy is a mosaic of shapes and colors formed by tall, living monarches, pointed spires of dead trees, angular crowns of young conifers and bright-green patches of broadleaf trees. — *Willamette National Forest, Oregon*
▼

The canopy collects water for storage in the trees' huge trunks and helps maintain the cool temperatures on the forest floor. Its cover also protects animals and streams from summer heat and shades delicate plants by serving as an umbrella from the strong sunlight. In winter, this tempering action provides warmth by acting as a thermal cover. The multiple layers of the canopy also protect the forest's soil. By intercepting rain before it hits the ground, the canopy helps prevent erosion and landslides.

In addition to collecting moisture, needles intercept chemicals carried by the wind and with the aid of microscopic fungi, transform these chemicals into valuable nutrients. Nitrogen is an important element contained in dust particles floating in the air. With the low level of nitrogen in most Pacific forest soils, air-bound nitrogen and other nutrients become a precious commodity.

Not only needles capture the sun's energy and moisture. Branches of ancient trees become aerial gardens of plants able to survive on chemical compounds carried by the air alone. The profusion of air plants growing on the ancient trees of the Olympic rain forest is unmatched by any other temperate rain forest in the world.

Specialized plants called *epiphytes* (*epi*, "upon"; *phyte,* "plant") take hold on the stout limbs of the upper canopy where light is maximum throughout the year. Though the canopy is not as rich in nutrients as is the forest floor, epiphytes forsake the ground for loftier aspirations. Unable to survive on the ground, these treetop dwellers draw their life support from rainfall, nitrogen leached from neighboring epiphytes and chemicals contained in dust particles.

The epiphytes most abundant in the Olympic rain forest include mosses, lichens, fungi, algae, liverworts and licorice fern. Epiphytes do not harm their hosts, nor rob them of food. Instead, they use them as a way to get closer to the water

and air which passes through the forest canopy. Special cells on their surface open when moisture is abundant and in order to conserve water, close tightly when the air becomes hot and dry. The prolific epiphytic plants of the forest canopy have adapted well to life in the treetops.

An important epiphyte of the Douglas fir forest canopy is a rather odd-looking lichen called *Lobaria oregana*. Light green, it resembles leaf lettuce and has a rubbery feel. Its primary task is to absorb and transform air-bound nitrogen. One of the most abundant lichens in ancient forests, lobaria attaches itself to twigs and branches in the upper canopy where it is closest to air and water. Researchers estimate the amount of lobaria growing on trees is at least four hundred pounds per acre. It is vital to forest maintenance and is nearly absent in forests younger than one hundred years.

Lobaria returns its full supply of nitrogen to the forest community in several ways. It is eaten by deer, elk and other animals who depend on the plant for the protein contained in them. Through their droppings, animals return some of the nutrients to the forest soil. Trapping more than it needs for normal growth, excess nitrogen in tree-bound lobaria is leached through rainfall. Seeping along a tree's trunk and branches, nitrogen is intercepted by other epiphytes or by the tree's own foliage. Rain, wind, snow and ice also dislodge lobaria,

▲
Animals need the protective cover created by the ancient forest canopy in both summer and in winter. By netting snow, the canopy forms a thermal cover under which animals can find food and stay sheltered from the cold.
— *Mt. Hood National Forest, Oregon*

Lofty ridges and precipitous slopes create a significant barrier to easterly moving moist air. Water laden clouds drop their loads in the form of rain or snow, ensuring a stable, wet environment on west facing slopes. — *Mt. Baker — Snoqualmie National Forest, Washington*

Numerous bird species use the conifer forest. Migrating hummingbirds follow spring blooms into the high mountains of the Pacific forest.

sending it to the ground where it decomposes, completing the cycle of nitrogen transfer.

As they grow, reproduce and die, epiphytes leave behind wastes which are attacked by decomposing bacteria and fungi. Soil is thus produced, albeit in small amounts, and builds up on tree branches underneath the thick mat of epiphytes. Some of this soil, dislodged by wind and rain, falls to the ground further aiding the humus buildup on the forest floor.

Soil anchored by epiphytes is also used in other ways. At least four species of deciduous trees — big leaf maple, black cottonwood, red alder and vine maple — develop aerial roots which tap the minerals contained under epiphytic

plants layering their branches. By raiding this rich resource, trees are able to supplement the diet provided by forest soils. From just above ground level to wherever epiphytes grow in dense mats, these broadleaf trees have been known to form roots up to three inches thick which trail several feet along their own branches.

The canopy feeds the forest, shelters its inhabitants and creates specialized homes for wild animals. Some spend their entire lives in the canopy, never touching the ground, yet contribute to the life below despite their distance. From the uppermost branches to the snags which pierce the mid-level and down to the lower branches out of the sun's reach, thousands of species of insects and 150 species of vertebrates

(including birds, fish, reptiles, amphibians and mammals) rely on the environment the canopy helps produce.

The highest branches represent the entire world for tiny creatures such as the red tree vole. Found nowhere else in the world, the red tree vole is the only mammal in North America that feeds exclusively on tree needles.

Researchers have found as many as fifteen hundred species of insects in the canopy of two ancient Douglas fir trees. Hundreds more live in the furrowed bark among mats of mosses and epiphytes on both twig and needle surfaces and on the accumulated debris caught among the branches. No one knows why there are so many species of insects in the canopies of rain forests, but that they exist in overwhelming abundance is certain.

Wide, heavy branches upholstered in cushiony epiphytes well out of reach of ground predators make ideal nests for birds. Yet the eggs and fledglings of these birds are preyed upon by martens and fishers who spend most of their time in arboreal pursuit of food.

The massive trunks of ancient trees, although limbless for hundreds of feet, provide hospitable environments. They, too, are home to a variety of animals including bats, who by day squeeze into the deeply fissured bark and by night feed on the thousands of insects inhabiting the canopy.

Snags, still-standing dead or dying trees, host several species of animals throughout their demise. Bats burrow under loose bark to sleep or bear young. Larger mammals, such as martens, bobcats and even bears make their sleeping and nesting dens in snags. They also are of particular importance to hole-nesting birds that use them for shelter in winter and rely on them for food throughout the year. Other birds, like the osprey, use the tops of snags almost exclusively for nesting. Because these animals are dependent upon each other and the homes they inhabit, they are severely affected by the

◄
The spotted owl lives only in the sheltered environment of the ancient forest canopy from southern British Columbia to northern California. An indicator species, its survival serves as a barometer for the overall health of the ancient forest.

◄
Like tropical rain forests, the Pacific rain forest hosts numerous epiphytic plants. Ferns, mosses and nitrogen-rich lichens cover the mid-canopy, forming soil on branches as they decay. Hardwoods take advantage of these extra soil nutrients by sending out aerial roots which crawl along their own branches.

►
Osprey utilize broken conifers tops along major waterways in the forest as nest sites. Their nests, platforms of sticks built over successive seasons, measure many feet in diameter. These lofty perches afford excellent viewing sites from which the osprey hunt.

►
Lobaria, a nitrogen-fixing lichen which grows on branches in the canopy, is a fungus that forms a symbiotic relationship with algae. In mutualistic symbiosis, the algae in lobaria provide food for the fungus through photosynthesis, and the fungus provides other kinds of nutrients as well as protection for the algae. Elk and deer forage on lobaria for its protein, especially in winter when other food sources are scarce. Lobaria does not grow in forests under 100 years of age.

loss of ancient forests.

The most notable endangered creature of the Pacific forests is the northern spotted owl. It seems ironic that a little-known and seldom-seen bird has become the symbol of the ancient forest. But this quiet, nocturnal predator inhabiting the forests from northern California to southern British Columbia was thrown into the spotlight because of its unique needs.

Northern spotted owls require the basic elements of old forests. Their nesting and breeding habits are dependent on the multi-layered canopy of old forests. Protection from the heat of summer and avoidance of predators is nearly guaranteed by the structure of old forests. In addition, by its mere presence the owl is indicative of the health of the forest. It epitomizes the cycle of life and the food chain typical in ancient forests.

This cycle, while built on numerous complex factors, is relatively simple. Owls eat small mammals which eat and disperse the spores of underground truffles and mushrooms. These fungi attach themselves to the roots of the trees, aiding their long life, which in turn creates the physical structure vital to the northern spotted owl. If one of these elements is removed, the cycle breaks. Because the owl sits figuratively at the top of this cycle, it has been chosen as an indicator species — the presence of the owl measures the health of the rest of the forest. The absence of owls could mean a permanent change in the forest as we now know it.

As much attention as the northern spotted owl has drawn, a rare, small and lesser-known bird has flown into the same spotlight because of its use of ancient forests — the marbled murrelet. A small, gray-brown, oblong-shaped bird, it feeds only in the ocean and nests only in ancient trees. Though known for some time, this sea bird remained an enigma because no one knew where it nested. It is one of the last birds in North

America to be carefully studied and is the only sea bird to nest so far into the ancient forest.

Following corridors formed by rivers and ravines, these small birds zip in and out of the forest once a day from April to July when they nest and fledge their young. After bobbing on waves and feeding in the surf for sand lance, herring and anchovies throughout the day, marbled murrelets vanish into the darkening forest. Their sharp, piercing call signals their presence as they streak through the forest at up to sixty miles per hour.

Large, flat, moss-lined branches as high as 165 feet in the air are perfect for the murrelet's nest. A small, dung-ringed depression is all that cradles the single egg laid each season. Where ancient forests edge the sea, marbled murrelets choose to nest closer to shore. But where extensive logging has occurred, the tiny bird must fly inland. One pair near Washington's Lake 22 flies fifty miles inland to find a suitable stand of large trees in which to give birth and shelter their young.

In 1854, upon ceding to the government his band's rights to live on the land as they had done for centuries, Chief Sealth (also known as Chief Seattle) implored the white people to have respect for the earth.

> Every part of the earth is sacred to my people. Every shining pine needle, every sandy shore, every mist in the dark woods, every clearing and humming insect is holy in the memory and the experience of my people. The sap which runs through the trees carries the memories of the red man. So we will consider your offer to buy our land. If we decide to accept, I will make one condition. The white man must treat the beasts of this land as his brothers. This we know. All things are connected like the blood of one family. All things are connected. Whatever befalls the earth befalls the sons of the earth. Man did not weave the web of life, he is merely a strand in it. Whatever he does to the web, he does to himself.

In an otherwise still landscape in Oregon's Opal Creek ancient forest, a

▶
The upper level of the forest is a latticework of conifer and broadleaf branches, filtering sun, buffeting winds and moderating temperatures in the hot summer months.
— *Mt. Baker/Snoqualmie National Forest, Washington*

▶
Rarely does sunlight touch the forest floor in great amounts. Rivers, however, form natural corridors of light through the canopy
— *Clackamas River Valley, Mt. Hood National Forest, Oregon*

Overleaf —
Autumn's fallen debris collects on the ground and in streams, increasing the nutrient base in the forest year after year. Cool temperatures in the Pacific forest prevent the quick breakdown of organic materials. Therefore, the forest floor consists of several layers of plant matter in all stage of decomposition.

▲
As its name implies, the
northern pygmy owl is tiny
— only six inches tall —
but it is ferocious. Hunting
by day in the shaded can-
opy, pygmy owls eat prey
such as insects, mice and
small songbirds.

tiny brown creeper silently threads the lines formed by the bark of a grizzled Douglas fir. Though perfectly camouflaged, he remains a strand in the web of life, all but hidden in his environment. As we consider Chief Sealth's words, we must remember that which is hidden from our gaze or, worse yet, has been lost because we have not honored his request. As the forest continues to reveal its secrets, like those of the northern spotted owl or the marbled murrelet, we finally begin to understand the connections Chief Sealth spoke of years ago.

Spring-blooming trilliums
are fed by generations of
organic matter which has
fallen from the canopy.
▼

FOOTSTEPS IN THE FOREST

◄

Stellar's jays are year-round
residents of the rain forest. Nearly 75% of all rain
forest bird species do not
make the long journey
south, but remain in the
forest throughout winter
months.

The temperate rain forest is unusually still. Decaying logs, carpets of
moss and fields of bracken create an
enchanting world of emerald greens and
maroon-browns. It's colorful and lumi-
nous, but hauntingly quiet. The gentle
melodies of wind and rain fill the air, but
the sounds of animals are scarce. Except
for the occasional ratchety voice of a
Steller's jay or the animated squabble of a
Douglas squirrel, it appears uninhabited.
Unlike a tropical rain forest, the temperate coniferous forest is a world of hushed silence, yet it is not without wildlife. In
reality, it is teeming with animal life
which has adapted to the multitude of
niches the forest has created.

Ultimately, all life on the planet
depends on the ability of plants to photosynthesize. In accord with their ability to
absorb and cleanse the air of excess carbon dioxide, plants replenish the earth
with oxygen, a vital component for all
living things. Forests are filled with
plants and huge trees capable of perpetu-
ating this cycle and are a critical link in
this process.

The sheer size as well as the longevity
of the trees within the ancient Pacific
forest creates a diverse structure which
provides numerous habitats. These settings are further shaped by the animals
which use these niches to their full
advantage. The forest community is a
product of the many concessions plants
and animals make with each other and as
a result, they develop interdependent
relationships.

Throughout the seasons, the forest
hosts various communities of animals

Chapter title page — Elk

◄

The maze of organic
material, living and dead,
littering the understory
offers niches for many
creatures. Rain forest
floors appear deceivingly
void of life to the unini-
tiated eye, falsely
supporting contentions
that the ancient forests
are unproductive. —
*Mt. Rainier National Park,
Washington*

which depend upon its seasonal
resources. Whether it is for food, nest
sites or shelter during harsh seasons, the
ancient forest nurtures its inhabitants
and in turn, they help perpetuate the
forest.

The number of animal species that
use the Pacific forest, either seasonally or
permanently, is astonishing. In western
Oregon and Washington, up to 110 mammal species are found. More bird families
live in that region than in any other area
in North America. The redwood and the
coastal rain forests of British Columbia
and southeast Alaska share some of these
varieties, and also harbor some indige-
nous species.

Some animals which live in the
greater Pacific forest can live in any type

◄
Various species of wild
salmon migrate upstream
to spawning beds
throughout the year. Once
exceptional in numbers,
wild stocks are now
depleted or extinct, due in
part to stream degradation
caused by clearcut logging
practices. — *Salmon River,
Mt. Hood National Forest,
Oregon*

of woodland as long as specific vegetation exists. Beavers, for example, need water and wood — commodities found in many ecosystems. Other animals require particular elements found only in ancient forests during certain seasons. The marbled murrelet, a sea bird, nests only in ancient forests. And others, such as the northern spotted owl, need the diverse structure only old forests can provide.

Although it is a temperate zone, the rain forest has identifiable seasons. Spring's soft rains bring stunning blossoms. Budding plants produce a palette of greens in every imaginable shade — each accentuated by light or shadow. Streams, swollen with rain and runoff from the high mountains, will dwindle when the summer drought hits. The killing frosts of autumn turn brilliant greens to somber ochre and the rains, absent for months, begin again. Winter is cool and dark, but the forest maintains its assort-

ment of color. Insipid mosses shine bright green even on dull, gray days.

Though not always in the foreground, elk, deer, raven, cougar, martens, voles, salamanders and a multitude of insects are found throughout the year, yet each has its season of full advantage. For many animals, winged and hooved alike, winter is the season of refuge within the rain forest.

Severe, cold winters rarely clutch the Pacific Coast. The climate is generally moderated by temperate, offshore oceanic currents, but on occasion frigid arctic air masses sweep down from Siberia and engulf the coast in an icy grip. During these winters, the insulating effect of the forest is critical to the survival of countless species. Temperatures may vary as much as ten degrees Fahrenheit between the inner and outer realm of the forest.

During extreme winters, the forest sways considerable influence on the ani-

▲
Vertical layering of the
rain forest structure dramatically increases
wildlife habitat for its
complex assemblage of
aerial inhabitants. Plat-
forms, branches and
spaces between ground
and canopy are home and
hunting territory for many
animals never seen. —
*Lady Bird Johnson Grove,
Redwood National Park,
California*

Once widespread through-
out the continent, elk are
now limited to mountain
areas and conifer forests
of the West. Those living
in the Pacific forest are
Roosevelt elk, slightly
larger than their cousins to
the east. They are named
for Theodore Roosevelt.
▼

mals which commonly seek the warmth, protection and food supply afforded within the interior of mature forests. The vaulted, multi-layered canopy of older forests ensures even the heaviest of snow-falls will be held aloft. The frozen moisture will be doled out as melting droplets nourishing the forest rather than blanketing it with an impenetrable barrier to creatures seeking refuge.

For elk and deer, the winter forest provides a bounty of lichens, mosses and bark on which to feed. In areas like the Hoh River valley of the Olympic National Park in Washington, the winter movements of a bull elk and his harem of females has become synonymous with the rain forest itself. While some of the resident elk follow retreating snow into the high country, others live year round in the lush rain-forested valley. A casual look at the understory reveals their signature browsing — ferns snipped short, plants stripped of leaves and woody shrubs clipped where new shoots should appear. The browse line marks the furthest extent to which the elk can reach as they pass through the forest in their nocturnal feeding expeditions. In heavy feeding areas, elk maintain the openness of the forest understory.

As spring approaches, the movement of elk and deer becomes more widespread and less dependent on the inner forest as new shoots and buds appear on the warmer fringes and in sun-washed meadows. During mild winters, the animals spend considerable time out from underneath the forest canopy. Behavioral notes taken during milder seasons lcd some researchers to speculate that hooved ruminants were better serviced in areas cleared of ancient forest. This misinterpretation of the evidence harbored only a portion of the truth. In areas of the Arctic where the forest has been extensively logged or damaged by natural fires or other calamities, the elk and deer populations pay heavy tolls.

Forage increases considerably in

▶
Deer populations have
increased dramatically
with the elimination of primary predators (wolves
and cougar) and the
expansion of browse habi-
tat as a result of intensive
logging. Though food
sources are abundant in
spring and summer, when
they are buried by snow in
winter, deer can starve or
suffer hypothermia in open
areas.

◀
Herds of elk residing
permanently in the west-
ern river valleys of the
Olympic Peninsula help
maintain an open
understory by browsing
on rain forest vegetation.
The resulting browse line,
the uppermost level at
which the animals can
feed, becomes clearly evident. — *Hoh River Valley,
Olympic National Park,
Washington*

▲

In early spring, the explosion of tender buds and shoots on deciduous trees and ferns draws wildlife into clearings and river edges to feed. — *Ten Mile Creek, Siuslaw National Forest, Oregon*

open areas and in summer, high-quality food can be abundant. But in winter, snows blanket these plentiful food sources and hooved animals are in danger of starvation and exposure to the cold. In addition, when trees growing in single-species plantations reach about thirty years of age, the canopy closes, squeezing out any light which fosters herbaceous plant or woody shrub growth. The floor of the forest remains dark and void of plants for nearly a century, providing little benefit to wildlife which depend on a natural forest for food, nesting and shelter.

In southeast Alaska's Tongass National Forest, snows can accumulate to depths of several feet covering all available forage in open spaces as well as the lower-elevation forest. Ancient groves become essential to the survival of the

Sitka black-tailed deer are not native to the Queen Charlotte Islands; they were imported as a food source at the beginning of the century. With few natural predators and plenty of browsing areas created by clearcutting, their population flourishes on this small chain of islands.

▼

◄
A common resident of the rain forest edge, great-horned owls are major predators of rare spotted owls and marbled murrelets.

◄
The reclusive marten is reflective of the fast-disappearing ancient rain forest. A beautiful cinnamon-colored member of the weasel family, the marten thrives in the varied canopy of the mature Pacific forest. It utilizes snags as dens for raising young and weathering winters.

Sitka black-tailed deer. In spring and summer, this subspecies of mule deer found only in the coastal rain forests of British Columbia and southeast Alaska, enter open high country. Because predatory bears have taken the low road to feed on salmon, the carefree Sitka black-tailed deer feed in meadows of wildflowers and deer cabbage.

As autumn approaches, they move to the outer edge of the forest, nibbling on shrubs which haven't yet lost their succulent leaves. Descending just ahead of the snow line, these small deer take refuge in the warmer, inner forest during the cold, wet winter.

Inside the columns of ancient Sitka spruce, luxuriant amounts of alectoria, or old man's beard lichen, drape branches and feather trunks in whispy gray-green strands. As winter storms and gusts of wind blow them wildly in all directions, alectoria and other lichens rain down from the upper canopy. The confetti of lichens provides a much needed supply of food, although low in nutrients, for the browsers who have diminished their supply of body fat by winter's end.

The woody debris scattered on the forest floor and free-standing snags play a critical role in the winter survival for many of the forest's smaller creatures. Snags offer a haven from the chill of winter for northern flying squirrels, Douglas squirrels, chipmunks and numerous mice species. For year-round resident birds, such as chickadees and brown creepers, snags are also essential to survival. A haven from the cold, snags also contain insects which provide much-needed protein lacking in winter. Even bears which spend most of the summer and autumn in the lowlands, need the collection of dead wood to survive. In winter, bears head to the high country and excavate dens under tree roots elevated over decaying nurse logs or at the base of decaying snags.

The massive trunks of fallen conifers

◄
Plunging silently into moss-covered branches, spotted owls prey on mice, tree voles and flying squirrels, mainstays of the rare owls' diet. Broad, short wings enable the owls to maneuver deftly through the maze of the canopy.

appear silent and lifeless, but within their rotting interiors life continues through the winter. The red-backed vole is architect and fabricator of a maze of tunnels beneath the soaked wood and organic debris of fallen trees. The vole's activity is driven by need as well as design. Like its aerial counterpart, the red tree vole, the red-backed vole has an appetite for a specific kind of food.

For the red-backed vole it is the truffle, the fruiting body of fungi which form the mycorrhizal associations with the roots of living conifers and other plants. In search of these underground delicacies, the vole burrows through a subterranean world during late fall and early winter when the truffles are at their zenith. Because truffles fruit underground and cannot depend on the wind to disperse their spores, they emit strong odors to attract voles and other mammals. In exchange for this culinary signal, animals spread the truffles' spores throughout the forest and into cleared areas where they begin the cycle anew.

The best place to spot the elusive fisher and its slighter cousin, the marten, is near decaying timber. Members of the weasel family, both are found in all ages of forest, although they often seek refuge in old forests during winter. The mass of fallen trees provides cover from predators such as the bobcat, cougar and great horned owl as well as from the cold. At the same time, small rodents, amphibians and invertebrates hiding within the woody debris provide a steady winter diet. Downed conifers are used both by fishers and martens as winter resting sites, although neither animal hibernates. In warmer months, both species will use snags to establish dens and feed on nesting chicks and eggs and on tree squirrels, their favorite prey.

In the spring, northern flying squirrels emerge from cavities in standing snags to feed on lichen, mushrooms and truffles and to court. The northern flying squirrel is an anomaly among its relatives. It is the only rodent to feed primarily on lichen. They are sometimes called the "darlings of the night," as no other rodent can claim to be quite as splendid. Huge round eyes, an adaptation for nocturnal activities, dominate a tiny face topped with alert ears.

Northern flying squirrels do not actually fly. They glide on flaps of skin which stretch when they extend their legs. Strictly nocturnal, they sail about the canopy with great precision. Flying squirrels often fall victim to spotted owls, great horned or great gray owls. As a primary defense, flying squirrels flip their tails in a direction opposite to their landing spot. As the would-be assailant strikes, it sometimes severs the tail, but the squirrel often escapes.

During the warming days of spring, the canopy becomes alive with flying insects and birds. The air is filled with the buzz and trills of aerial songsters. Insects are awakened by the lengthening rays of the sun and by the aroma of a myriad of blossoms. In turn, avians are attracted by the invertebrate feast. Songbirds venturing from winter homes in the tropical rain forests take advantage of this seasonal feast as they migrate to the northern forests to breed and raise their young.

A common misconception is that these birds — warblers, vireos, swifts, orioles, tanagers and flycatchers — are residents of the north which fly south for the winter to escape the cold and to find food. But it isn't so. The songbirds are actually residents of the tropics who leave their homes and travel thousands of miles to nest in the northern forests, a far safer environment.

The northern forests do not have better food resources than the lush tropical rain forest. Day length in the tropics is equal throughout the year, but day length in the north is longer in the summer and birds simply have more time to hunt. Therefore, they can gather more food for their chicks. In addition, nest predation

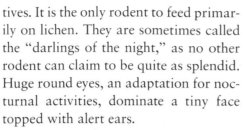
Bears feed ravenously on salmon. During peak salmon runs in Alaska's Tongass region, bears congregate in unusually large numbers and feast on dozens of fish every day.

in the tropics is much higher than in the temperate region.

In winter, many non-songbirds also leave the north for warmer latitudes. One such bird, one that depends on the ancient Pacific forest, is the Vaux's swift. Swifts are amazing flyers and spend most of their lives in the air. Their bodies are streamlined for aerial pursuit. Long, curved wings, a short, stubby tail and a thin, cigar-shaped body make them fast and agile. Gliding and wheeling through the air, they are adept at hunting moths, mosquitos, flies and other insects. Swifts are so adapted to life in the air that they can barely walk on their tiny feet. When at rest or nesting, swifts cling to the sides of vertical surfaces with the help of bare shafts at the ends of their feathers.

Unlike their eastern cousin, the chimney swift, Vaux's swifts have not taken to nesting outside of the coniferous forest to which they migrate each spring. Instead, groups of Vaux's swifts fly for thousands of miles from their homes in South America and continue to search for snags, typically found in the dwindling habitat of the ancient forests. When they find snags, they build stick nests attached by saliva to the inside vertical surface of dead trees often hollowed out by fire. As habitats in both the tropical and temperate forests are decimated, they will become extinct like other animals dependent on these ancient forests.

Adding to the complexity of the forest are animals revered by Native Americans as master builders. Honored for their natural carpentry skills, beavers were often carved onto totems lining the entryways of longhouses. It is easy to understand native peoples' reverence for these large rodents. In a world without chainsaws, diesel-powered machinery or trucks, beavers effortlessly toppled large trees and used every bit of them for their existence.

In the foothills of Mt. Rainier in Washington's Cascade Range, a stream coerced into widening its banks by a

◄
Visiting the low elevation forests in winter to feed and to avoid inclement weather, mountain goats were hunted by Native Americans. As the animals shed in the spring, tufts of wool were deposited on sticks and rough tree bark. Collected by Indian women, the highly-prized wool was woven into blankets coveted as a valuable trade item.

◄
Beavers are the only creatures other than humans that intentionally alter the forest. Downed trees in the wake of their nightly forays add to the ever-changing face of the forest community. The flooded margins of a beaver pond become home to wood ducks, buffleheads, woodpeckers and a host of insect-eating songbirds.

family of beavers winds its way through a tiny island of ancient forest. The detour seems to have little affect on the stream's flow, but the grove of trees which once stood along the banks of the stream have been gnawed into an ever-widening circle.

Animals depend on the forest and the forest depends on its animal inhabitants. Through seed and fungal spore dispersal and other forest-building acts, animals assist themselves and each other in maintaining the hospitable environment of the ancient Pacific forests.

White-footed voles, red tree voles and Larch Mountain salamanders could not exist anywhere else. Others, such as fishers, martens and dusky-footed woodrats, would be hard pressed to find homes elsewhere. Even elk, whose numbers once reached ten million across the continent, have been reduced to a mere five hundred thousand.

Animals at the top of the food chain always suffer first from destruction of habitat and food sources. Cougar, bobcat and lynx have become scarce in the coastal forest. Salmon runs have declined drastically, and some native species have already been lost to extinction.

At one time, the Pacific forest and its inhabitants were safe. It existed in harmony and maintained its populations at levels the environment could sustain. But as humans, a species which does not maintain its population at a sustainable level, moved across the continent, animals and native peoples lost their homes quickly and, for some, permanently.

The small parcel of the original, ancient Pacific forest which remains is the last refuge for communities of animals that have existed for thousands of years. If this vulnerable region isn't protected and preserved, it soon will be without these animals which enrich and perpetuate the life of the forest upon which humans, too, are dependent.

▲
Snow rarely covers the ground in the ancient forest. This leaves valuable winter forage available for animals who find refuge there during the cold months. — *Mt. Rainier National Park, Washington*

▲

Historically widespread
throughout North America,
cougars have been forced
to exist in islands of wilderness along the Pacific
Coast. Usually these wil-
derness islands are
surviving patches of tem-
perate rain forest.

◄

Inhabiting the northern
reaches of the Pacific forests, the great gray owl
prefers conifer stands,
bogs and meadows where
it hunts primarily by day.
Not commonly seen even
in the heart of its range,
this owl is the largest of
the North American spe-
cies, standing 24 to 33
inches tall.

AN EVERGREEN OASIS

t was the most magical bird naturalist John Muir ever watched. He sat near the sounds of waterfalls and streams and witnessed the comings and goings of the musical water ouzle "living a charmed life." The size of a robin, the ouzel "sings a sweet, fluty song all winter and all summer, in storms and calms, sunshine and shadow, haunting the rapids and waterfalls with marvelous constancy," said Muir, adding that the flutelike voice had "love in it."

The water ouzle, or dipper, is water given life with wings, "building his nest in the cleft of a rock bathed in spray. He is not web-footed, yet he dives fearlessly into foaming rapids." Searching the world over, one could never find two so inextricably bound as the water ouzle and its cascading partner. "Bird and stream, one and inseparable," said Muir.

In the confines of the rain forest, light struggles to penetrate and the plants which flourish are adept in their means of securing light. Where the forest opens, life congests in exuberance. Along waterways, sunshine pours in and the chaotic assortment of plants soak up every measure of light. Where rivers form glistening ribbons through deep canyons, the ouzle flies, "seeming to take the greater delight in the more boisterous the stream, always as cheerful and calm as any linnet in a grove," wrote Muir.

The streams which thread the Pacific forest tie the land to the sea in an inseparable relationship. Nowhere on the continent are the forest and its inhabitants more dependent upon water. Vast tracts of conifers blanket the cold polar regions and arid inner mountains of western North America, but the land between the mountains of the West Coast and the waves of the Pacific holds a forest spawned by the warm, damp breath of the sea. Whether by supporting trees, water ouzels or orca whales, the water courses through the Pacific forest and affects the lives of a multitude of species of plants and animals.

On any given day in the Pacific coast rain forest, the odds are four to one that water will fall in one form or another. Whether it's mist, snow or fog, water always relinquishes to the forces of gravity. On nearly every day of the year, the rain forest is either absorbing moisture or releasing it.

The origin of the water passing through or taking refuge in the forest depends on where one starts. Like the streams and rivers in which it flows, water is on a perpetual journey without beginning or end. Cycling from sea to

◄ Thousands of rivers and streams thread the rain forest. They provide critical habitat to a wide variety of creatures, particularly amphibians such as newts, frogs, toads and salamanders. — *Fire Creek, Mt. Baker/ Snoqualmie National Forest, Washington*

Chapter title page — Rain on red alder leaf

Muskeg rain forests in southeast Alaska form a unique wetland habitat for waterfowl, bears and moose. Vast insect blooms around the muskegs in midsummer provide a rich protein supply for migratory songbirds. — *Revillagigedo Island, Alaska*
▼

▲
**Water cascading over
small and large falls is a
quintessential element of
the Pacific Coast rain
forest.** — *Fire Creek, Mt.
Baker/ Snoqualmie National
Forest, Washington*

land to shore with moments in the glaciers, rivers, tree trunks, ponds, bogs and
estuaries, water pauses but never truly
stops.

Surging tides disperse water onto
beaches marked with the tiny footprints
of a thousand shore birds. Rain falls onto
the great trees of the forest and
replenishes them as it has for thousands
of years. Buoyant fog envelopes the broken canopy and is captured by millions of
needles. It then drips to the mosses, ferns
and lichens growing on the upper limbs
and continues on a long journey down a
three hundred foot-tall trunk. Snow-
banks irrigate slopes blanketed with
alpine flowers. Melting glaciers send
their water down icy avenues of feeder
streams which tumble down canyon

walls and explode into a fine spray before
joining a swift stream. Water from
underground rivers formed by volcanic
processes surfaces and cascades over
steep falls. It flows to the ocean, to be
swept up in an eternal dance with time.

The forest serves as a reservoir for
the bulk of this moisture. The enormous
conifers are virtual water towers, holding
two thousand gallons and more. In the
coastal rain forests, fallen logs, wet soil
and prodigious ground cover hold
enough moisture to lessen the devastating effects of fire. Roots anchor steep
slopes and keep erosion in check, and
serve as a watershed protector by regu-
lating the amount of water seeping into
the streams and rivers.

In the redwoods, the trees themselves

▲
Sediments, debris and other residue deposited along river banks after heavy spring runoffs provide fertile nurseries for an assortment of water-dependent land plants. —
Lewis River, Washington

help create a microclimate totally dependent on water. Through the process of transpiration, a single tree returns five hundred gallons of water per day into the atmosphere through its millions of needles. As the coastal fog, so common to this region, collides with this wall of moisture released from the redwoods, rain forms and replenishes the soil with the water which will eventually continue the cycle of life. A morning walk among the earth's largest trees often is a wet one. But the rain isn't from the sky, it is from fog dripping off the great conifer's needles.

Water in the Pacific forest doesn't only come down from the sky. Under the forests cloaking the mountains of the Pacific region, water boils up from the

depths of the earth. Hundreds of hot springs spew thermal spring water warmed by volcanic action below. Hot springs form as surface water seeps down to lower levels in the earth through fractures and the loosely formed volcanic soil typical of this region. It is heated and pushed back up through cracks in warm underground rocks.

Steeped in dissolved minerals leached from surrounding rocks, hot springs have captivated man's imagination throughout history. Rising with the ash-gray steam are Native American myths and legends about their powers. From the cauldron below the igneous rock, great fires spawned the Olympic peninsula and also spawned a story of the creation of two such springs.

▶ Bathed by fog and mist most of the year, the coastal forest relies on moisture built up over the Pacific Ocean and pushed ashore by steady winds. Damp soils, downed logs and living trees retain a high percentage of this water, which is released slowly during drier months. — *Hoh River Valley, Olympic National Park, Washington*

◄

Spectacular waterfalls play a vital role in producing aerial moisture in the form of mist. Canyons, gorges and rock walls become enclaves for rare plants and animals seeking relief from the heat of summer. — *Elowah Falls, Columbia Gorge National Scenic Area, Oregon*

▲
Coastal rain forest floors provide a rich, competitive nursery of water-soaked mosses and humus from which young plants emerge. Even on hot summer days, the soil beneath the top layer of moss remains cool and damp.

◄
Volcanoes and pressure faults in the earth's crust have contorted the Pacific coastal landscape into a place of austere beauty. Cascading water follows splits and fissures in the rock which hasten its return to the ocean. — *Opal Creek, Oregon*

▶
Water is a crucial element in the cycling of nutrients within the forest.

Overleaf —
The proliferation of life along streams and rivers creates a green clutter reminiscent of a tropical rain forest. Plants unable to live inside the shaded forest thrive on the river banks where the sun pours in. — *Tanner Creek, Columbia Gorge National Scenic Area, Oregon*

By late summer, streams which flooded their banks with spring rains recede to a gentle flow. In summer, much of the water released to streams is from the reservoir stored in the forest system. — *Quartz Creek, Dark Divide Proposed Wilderness, Washington*
▼

▲

Snow melt and spring rain turn quiet waterways into torrents of white water. — *Upper Clackamas River, Mt. Hood National Forest, Oregon*

Up through the lush rain forest of the northern peninsula rise the Sol Duc and Olympic hot springs. The Klallam people believed that two dragons, Sol Duc and Elwha, fought a fierce and unparelleled battle. In the end, neither could subdue the other. They returned to their lairs, sealed them shut and wept in bitter defeat. Their tears formed the steamy springs which today are used by people who believe in the magical curative properties of the boiling waters.

The water that forms the backbone of the Pacific forest travels through diverse terrain. Whether cascading over steep walls, settling in a beaver-made pond, trickling down a watershed, pooling in the cradle of a natural alpine ampitheater or mingling with salt water in an estuary, water permeates every layer, every surface. Animals adapted to a watery life and found a unique refuge in each of these habitats.

Occupying a special niche in the saturated forest is a family of animals which uses both bodies of water and the wet forest floor in order to survive. Amphibians hatch and breed in streams and revert to a terrestrial life in between. Wet winters, cool summers, a soaked floor and plenty of streams or pools assure a fruitful existence for amphibians.

▶

Increasingly rare, giant Douglas firs of 500 to 1,000 years in age are critically important water reservoirs in the dry summer ecology of the forest. Trunks 5 to 8 feet in diameter and towering in excess of 300 feet safeguard thousands of gallons of water. — *Cathedral Grove, Vancover Island, B.C.*

For reptiles, though, the perpetually cool atmosphere of the Pacific coastal forest is limiting. As a result, most of the Pacific forest is void of snakes, turtles and lizards, but is abundant with newts, frogs, toads and salamanders.

The Siskiyou Mountains, untouched by the glaciers that etched most of the Pacific forest, are filled with innumerable tarns, ponds and bogs. Some are formed after fall rains or as spring runoff replenishes soft depressions in the land. In these ancient waterways, several species of amphibians are surrounded by a diversity of plant life surpassed only by that found in the Great Smoky Mountains. Though not as numerous as plants, the diversity of amphibians found throughout the Pacific forest is wide.

Because their skin lacks an effective moisture barrier, amphibians do not venture far from water or from the protective moist cover of logs and other debris littering the forest floor. In spring, Ash Swamp in the northern Siskiyou forest is filled with the croaking sound of thousands of frogs. Newts, emerging from their warmer underground sanctuaries, crawl back to their boggy hatching ground. Along the bank of Babyfoot Creek nestled in the Siskiyou's Kalmiopsis Wilderness, the endemic giant Pacific salamander, measuring up to a foot long, patrols the damp recesses created by rocks lining the stream for insects, smaller salamanders and even small mice and garter snakes.

Flowing through corridors of strong, living trees and cascading over their fallen brethren, the streams and rivers of the Pacific forest are also birthing dens and hatcheries for the most productive salmon runs in the world. Switching from fresh to salt water and back to fresh again in a lifetime exacts a tremendous toll. The wild salmon require tributary waters of great purity and diverse structure.

Streams provide a multitude of diverse habitats for fish where the ancient

◄
In late fall and early spring, numerous animals congregate along waterways to feed on fish. Along these waterways, wildlife viewing is at its best.

◄
Water bathes the Pacific forest for most of the year. The northern reaches receive more moisture than those in the south, but all are washed in rain, snow or fog. — *Hoh River Valley, Olympic National Forest, Washington*

rain forest has never been disturbed by human interference and has been left to regenerate under its own direction. Roots of living trees hold riverbanks in place. If not for them, swift running water would cut wider and deeper channels into the surrounding soil. Fallen trees create the calm, gravel-lined beds which salmon seek for spawning. Aging quickly, adult salmon returning to fresh water rest in the placid pools created by log jams before they attempt another great leap upstream. Once hatched, the tiny fry feed on insects and hide from predators

in such pools. The disorderly array of logs lining the river bank form a crossing to the other side and pile up against each other and further assist the fish as they create deep plunge pools and stretches of fast flowing riffles. Both are necessary for salmon who must have a wall of force and turbulent waters to work against.

In a cycle as old as the forest itself, salmon obey a timeless impulse to return to the conifer-lined streams in which they were hatched to mate, lay eggs and eventually die. In nature's last attempt to insure survival of the fittest, only the

Shelf fungus
▼

119

strongest will make it into the shallow pools to pass on their genes to the next generation.

These and other fish, including sturgeon and some trout, are anadromous (*ana*, "upward"; *dromous*, "running"), meaning that although they are hatched and die in the freshwater streams sheltered by the ancient forest, their life in between is spent in the sea. Forest streams are safe hiding places for eggs and the tiny fry which subsequently hatch are able to hide from predators. But soon insects, their major food source, can not sustain them.

The ocean, with its rich supply of plankton and herring, is a more hospitable and nutritious place. Within a year, young salmon migrate downstream and enter the cold waters of the Pacific Ocean. Depending on the species, salmon live from two to five years in the ocean. Huge migrations follow the coastline. Chinook salmon travel along the edge of the continental shelf from San Francisco Bay to Alaska — a twenty-five hundred mile trip.

Feeding on fish and shellfish, salmon grow to an enormous size. Twenty-five percent of a female salmon's body weight is her ovaries, which helps to explain how salmon produce thousands of eggs.

Gathering at the mouthes of streams and rivers, shoals of salmon provide an easy source of food for larger marine animals. One of the largest of these underwater predators is the orca whale. Migrating along the same routes as

▲
Unstable soils, high winds and plentiful amounts of rain contribute to natural landslides. These open areas are usually colonized by shrubs and deciduous broadleaf trees.
— *Upper Clackamas River, Mt. Hood National Forest, Oregon*

▲
Rough-skinned newts
spend more time in the
water than any other newt
in the Pacific forest.

salmon, pods of orca, or killer whales, feast on salmon during the spring and summer runs. Orcas live in oceans around the globe, but prefer cooler waters and those plentiful in food.

While they do consume other kinds of fish, including other whales and even marine mammals, the abundant salmon runs of the Pacific coastal forests provide a rich seasonal feast. Families of ten to fifty orcas consist of one adult male, several females and their offspring. They forage along the coast and into sidewaters looking for salmon. Hunting as a group, they herd the fish into small inlets where they are systematically removed from the water.

Orcas are the largest members of the dolphin family and are unmistakable in the water. Males can grow to over thirty feet long. Six-foot-tall dorsal fins rise out of the placid waters of the Pacific Ocean. Striking black and white bodies contrast the blue water and the green backdrop of the forest. In play or in communication, an orca will jetison out of the water, twist, turn completely over and slap the surface with its enormous body. Water sprays in angular sheets as the whale disappears into the depression created by its thick body.

In the Puget Sound, the Straight of Georgia, the Straight of Juan de Fuca and into Queen Charlotte Sound, live twenty pods made up of 250 individuals. Identified by underwater sounds, they stay close to shore, mating, giving birth and trolling the water for food. The resident

◄
Moisture collects on the millions of needles covering the conifer trees of the ancient forest. Fog drip is a major contributor of water in forest soils and streams.

orcas symbolize the vitality of the streams and rivers which pass through the forest and, in turn, the forest itself. Without the forest, these waterways would not harbor the abundance of life which orcas and countless other marine mammals and sea birds depend upon.

Slipping past the orcas which hug the coastline, salmon become prey to other marine mammals. Seals and sea lions along the rocky shores of the Pacific forest consume vast amounts of salmon. Gliding among them, these excellent swimmers torpedo through the water, aided by their streamlined bodies and strong flippers.

Entering a shoal of salmon, seals and sea lions nab fish with powerful jaws and teeth designed solely for tearing. Seals and sea lions gather by the hundreds at the mouths of Pacific forest rivers to fish for salmon, much to the consternation of fishermen in strong competition with these quick and agile animals.

Escaping the great orcas and slipping past the vigilant sea lions, the salmon which make it upstream have yet another predator to face — bears. Lumbering down from the rain forest mountains where they feed on berries, shrubs and bugs, bears camp on the sides of coastal rivers and eat to their heart's content. Only along the rivers will bears congregate in numbers — an unusual behavior, except during the salmon runs. Bears generally forage by themselves but will tolerate each other along the riverbanks where food is more than plentiful.

On Pace Creek on Admiralty Island in the Tongass National Forest, the phenomenon of salmon running upstream, combined with the spectacle of bears fishing together, followed by sea gulls looking for scraps, is magnificent. No matter how many bears line the riverbank, each one has a different fishing style.

There are waders, who walk out into the shallows and wait for a salmon to pounce upon. There are grabbers, who walk out a little further and grab the nearest fish with their paws. The rock-hopping chompers are the most amusing. Tiptoeing along rocks which form rapids, the chomper will stand at attention waiting for a salmon to make a surging leap. When it does, he nabs the fish in its jaws.

An aerial predator watches the entire scene. Bald eagles evoke such strong emotions that it is difficult to believe such a magnificent animal is a scavenger. In the proximity of open water, both fresh and marine, the stately bald eagle surveys its watery kingdom. Its unmistakable cries command the attention of every forest denizen as it soars the thermal currents rising from the forest. But while the alabaster-crowned patriarch of Indian totems is a proficient hunter itself, it often eats the discards and remains of others. The bald eagle feeds on spent salmon lining rain forest river banks. In its more graceful moments, it will glide above a river and with exacting efficiency, plunge just below the surface with outstretched talons to pluck a fresh fish from icy water.

The bald eagle is the largest avian of the Pacific forest. Its nest of twisted sticks and conifer boughs is equally magnificent. Built over a decade, the platform perched atop a canopy-erupting snag is not difficult to see but is difficult to find. Bald eagles, the symbol of strength and power chosen by the United States of America, have struggled in recent years. Deforestation and aquatic pollutants have exacted their toll on this supreme predator. Fortunately, in the vicinity of the coastal rain forests, a fragment of their historic majesty remains.

Along the southernmost tip of the Queen Charlotte Islands gather the greatest concentration of bald eagles in Canada. In the South Moresby Island Wilderness, the symbol of wildness that once prevailed throughout the watery regions of the entire North American continent finds refuge. These streams,

▲
Pods of orca whales consist of one mature male, several females and their offspring. Though female babies stay in their resident pod, males eventually form pods of their own.

rivers and intertidal zones of islands are the last sanctuary for many species of wildlife. Abolished or endangered throughout most of its former range, here the bald eagle thrives, as it does along much of the north coast.

Drenched by the never-ending deluge of rain and ocean tides, the Queen Charlotte Islands epitomize the connection between forest and water. Perhaps nowhere else along the length of the Pacific Coast does this connection seem so natural and so eternal. Surrounded by the icy Pacific, the islands are a sanctuary for many species found nowhere else in the world. Separated from the mainland by fifty miles, life on the Queen Charlotte Islands developed in isolation. Made up of a multitude of habitats, the islands are home to animals which evolved over millions of years.

The element which builds the forest and sculpts the land also shapes life for a multitude of animals which live within the cycle of water in the Pacific forest. Only the rain forests of the tropics are equally as dependent on the wash of sea-born moisture. Like the temperate rain forests, they are connected to the eternal tides of rain, fog and mist.

In the past, observers shortsightedly defined the role of water in the rain forest by that which was most obvious — rain and the precipitant rivers. As the complex roles of fog, mist, snow and boggy lowlands are discovered, vision improves.

Orca whales live in the waters edging the Pacific forest. They often follow salmon runs, feeding on the fish returning to their steam or river of origin.

▼

The Totem's Tale

Look at me, friend!
I come to ask for your dress.
You have come to take pity on us,
for there is nothing for which you can not be used,
because it is your way that there is nothing
for which we can not use you,
for you are really willing to give us your dress.
I come to beg you for this, Long Life Maker,
for I am going to make a basket for lily roots out of you.
I pray, friend,
to tell your friends what I ask of you.
Take care friend.
Keep sickness away from me so that I may not be killed
in sickness or in war, O friend.

— Kwakiutl woman speaking to redcedar, wanting to pull back its bark.

The coastal rain forests which nuzzle countless bays, straits and inlets along the Pacific Coast are peaceful and serene settings. Occasionally, seals haul out on shorelines where turnstones and assorted peeps work the water's edge for a meal. Sooty oystercatchers ply the debris of a recent storm for the treasure awaiting beneath a kelp blade or sea shell. Their raucous voices interrupt the serenity.

A century past, these sea margins were alive with the soft, melodic voices of Haida Indian women and children as they collected clams, limpets and other marine creatures in baskets made of cedar bark and roots. Native Americans lived and thrived in communities along the Pacific Coast.

From the Gulf of Alaska down the British Columbian coast and into Washington and Oregon, the Tlingit, Nootka, Quilliut, Salish and Bella Coola bands lived in harmonious existence between the rain forest and the sea. For each of the seven major coastal peoples, a tale of origin linked the two dominant forces in their lives and told of their love and need for the sanctuary of their environment.

A vestige of the great Haida people lives on the Queen Charlotte Islands, an enchanting archipelago of mountaintops rising from the sea fifty miles off the north coast of British Columbia. They are talented seafarers and masters of living in harmony with the islands' lush and bountiful rain forests.

In the legend of their creation, the Haida explain how their people were freed from a giant clam shell by a curious and jester-like raven. Raven Yel was amused by the featherless creatures. Soon after their release, the people escaped into the nearby rain forest. There they learned all that was important and valuable in living. Their reverence for the forest strengthened the fabric of the people and fashioned the Haida ethic of living compatibly within their rich and bountiful environment.

Today, the traditional life of the Haida, like all the traditional people of the Pacific coastal rain forest region, is only a memory. Mere fragments remain of a people who possessed tremendous skill and pride in their ability to live and

◄
Remnants of native settlements dot the northern shores of America's rain forest. Totems tell the tale of these people's connection to the land. These resourceful natives no longer inhabit the forest in traditional communities. All that is left at the old village sites are decaying totems. Their stories of the sea, the animals, and the people who were linked to them are returning to the earth. — *Skedans, Queen Charlotte Islands, B.C.*

Chapter title page — **Totem detail** — *Skidegate Band Council longhouse, Queen Charlotte Islands, B.C.*

◄

With the European and
Russian traders in the late
1700s came metal-bladed
tools which made carving
easier. Indians used their
new possessions to carve
totem poles and other
objects decorated with figures which symbolized
their family heritage. —
Museum of Anthropology,
University of British
Columbia

131

► For thousands of years, Native Americans had no written symbols to record their stories. History was woven into legends and song and taught to children until they could repeat it and carry it to the next generation. — *Museum of Anthropology, University of British Columbia*

Decades of coastal weather have reduced totems to ghostly reminders of a people who once flourished among the riches of the rain forest. — *Skedans, Queen Charlotte Islands, B.C.* ▼

in concert with the land. Like the fast-disappearing traditional people of tropical rain forests, the cultures of America's Pacific rain forests were keepers of the ways and means to unlock the secrets of the forest without destroying the very place where those secrets were hidden.

Near Anthony Island, off the southern tip of South Moresby Island in the Queen Charlottes, the marine waters are often calm. Their depths are crystalline to over fifty feet. Sea stars of terra-cotta and crimson decorate the rocky seams and bulges. Orcas, the great killer whales, cruise the waters in their formal black and white attire. From above, bald eagles in the peaks of three-hundred-foot-tall Sitka spruce trees keep a watchful eye on the ebb and flow of life.

Approaching from the sea, a protected cove reveals Ninstints, an ancient Kunghit Haida village. A few feet from the water's edge, tremendous carved totems stand frozen in formation. Their graphic faces are wooden interpretations of the Haida world. Their western red cedar hulks are weathered ash-gray. Crevasses of time have split their lengths and for many, the surrounding rain forest has begun to reclaim that which it lent to the people of Ninstints twelve decades earlier.

For the traditional people of the

Pacific Coast rain forests, the wealth of the land was nearly utopian. Though they were not completely free from hardship and suffering, life seemed eternally fruitful between the sea and the rain forest. Of all the forest plants and animals woven into the fabric of traditional rain-forest life, the the stately western redcedar was dominant. While many forest trees, shrubs and other plants found their way into Indian culture, it remained the cedar on which the various peoples built their survival and heritage.

In mature Pacific Coast rain forest, idyllic western redcedars are the quintessential temperate rain forest monarchs. Their massive trunks consistently measure twenty feet or more in diameter and vault nearly three hundred feet into the canopy. Graceful *J*-shaped limbs and lace-work leaves resemble fog and mist in botanical form. Few living things on earth compare in mass and age. Perhaps no other tree on the Pacific Coast embodies the American rain forest and the beauty and reverence the native people saw in such grand trees.

For a thousand years or more, these grizzled giants have listened to the crashing Pacific Ocean, felt the salt breeze and witnessed a thousand generations of salmon returning from the sea to fight their way up the coastal creeks. Cedars of such age and wisdom spoke to the Indians and in turn, they respected the great trees.

In the tale of the western redcedar by the Coast Salish people of Washington's Olympic Peninsula, there lived a good man who was always helping others. He provided whatever they needed, be it tools, clothing or shelter. When the Great Spirit saw this, he said, "That man has done his work; when he dies and where he is buried, a cedar tree will grow and be useful to the people: the roots for baskets, the bark for clothing, the wood for shelter."

The extent to which coastal bands took advantage of the rain forest is aston-

ishing. From the western redcedar alone, they made more than two hundred tools and artifacts. Among them were dozens of basket styles, bark boxes, totems, canoes, longboats, ladles, combs, baby cradles, clothing, bark rain hats, and the spiritual and mystical longhouses. The natives shaped the redcedar with fire, steam, pressure, weight and blade into every conceivable daily article.

In traditional culture, the bond of rain forest and sea runs deep. While in ecological terms these lush, emerald forests depend on the sea, the bands of the Pacific Coast saw the two as individual parts of the whole. Salmon and cedar were prime partners in this union of different worlds. What a thirty-pound fish

◀

Thousands of village sites
mark the end of a way of
life for coastal people
whose populations are
still strong. While many of
the early totem poles have
been sent to museums and
others fade with the years,
all have become inspira-
tion to new generations of
native carvers and craftsmen who carry on the
traditions of their ancestors.
— *Skedans, Queen
Charlotte Islands, B.C.*

exploring the depths of the icy Pacific and a towering community of conifers have in common seems obscure. For the coastal people, the two shared much, and as historians and ecologists are now learning, they depended on both.

A generation of salmon, depending on the species, develops every three to five years. An odyssey begins from the day the wriggling fry shake free their birth bubbles and begin to explore the outer reaches of their river nursery. Anadromous, salmon venture downstream and transition into the salt water of the Pacific as fingerling-sized juveniles. For the next few years, they grow and feed in the rich ocean waters before returning en masse to the rivers and streams of their origin. There the cycle begins anew as salmon spawn another generation and die.

Without exception, the seven major native American bands looked upon the salmon with great respect. Myth, legend and religion among the various people created a spectrum of tales, but the belief was consistent that salmon were eternal sea people disguised in the fins and scales of fish.

Emerging from the great-ocean house in the spring, the salmon were sent forth to fill the forest rivers and provide a bounty of food for the people. Reverence for this wonderful fish was not only achieved through salmon prayers, but was also acted out in strictly prescribed rituals. Salmon skeletons were returned in their entirety to the water, as they believed that once in the sea the salmon's spirit would change back into a person and then the following spring, into a fish once more.

The salmon/cedar connection was more than ecological. People turned to the forest to provide many of the tools with which to catch salmon. Once again, western redcedar was the tree of choice. Other species from the forest family — Pacific yew, Sitka spruce, western hemlock and Douglas fir — were commonly incorporated into objects of art and purpose. Indians created hooks, traps and weirs, along with nets to catch salmon, halibut, herring, cod, smelt, sturgeon and euchalon.

Each of these fish assumed its rightful place in the various bands' lives. Salmon was significant to everyone. For the seafaring bands like the Haidas and Tlingits, deep-water cod and halibut were also vital food sources.

By the time the first Russian and European explorers found their way to the coastal region in the eighteenth century, the native bands had developed a civilization based on the forest and the sea. From southeast Alaska, the Tlingits were trading their Chilkat mountain goat blankets as far south as the Puget Sound and the Olympic Peninsula. Shorter routes of commerce between the Nootka, Kwakiutl and Salish, and the Tsimshian and Haida were common.

Each of the seven major bands became noted for artistic and utilitarian specialties. Coast Salish were worthy basket makers as well as weavers of blankets of mountain goat and dog hair. The seafaring Haidas built beautiful canoes.

While the Haida mastered the art of open-ocean boat building, Coast Salish bands in the protected waters of the Puget Sound refined open canoe design. Lofty, straight-grained conifers provided exceptional building materials. "The Giant Tree of Life," as the redcedar's Latin name indicates, was a tree of many uses.

Peoples with basic hand tools fash-

▲
Totems-turned-nurse-logs are barely recognizable to all but the trained eye. Sites where totems were removed, stolen or burned by missionaries can be identified by the stinging nettle and crabapple trees which still grow there. Chiefly hunter-gatherers, native people grew few food crops; stinging nettle was grown only for weaving rope.

ioned tremendous wooden articles: massive ocean canoes, totems and longhouses. The nature of the redcedar — clear, easily-split grain; strong and light weight — enhanced these creations. Native wooden construction shocked and amazed the early European explorers.

In numerous villages, central longhouses measuring forty by one hundred feet were common. Soaring cathedral-like interiors boasted plank roofs supported by a single-length leviathan of red cedar two to four feet in diameter.

Navigating the coast in 1788, Captain John Meares entered these remarks in his ship's journal:

> The trees that supported the roof were of a size which would render the mast of a first-rate man of war diminutive, on a comparison with them; indeed our curiosity as well as our astonishment was on its utmost stretch, when we considered the strength that must be necessary to raise these enormous beams to their present elevation; and how such strength could be found by a people wholly unacquainted with mechanical powers.

In traditional coastal life, the village faced the water, but security rested in the backyard. Extending skyward behind the totems and longhouses, straight trunks from the best trees formed the framework of a great house. A main beam dominated the construction but was merely the spine of a truly marvelous architectural creation. Tandem ridge beams paralleled the main beam and were often fluted. In the typical house of a prominent chief, the beams protruding through the front wall sported carvings of animal spirits. Marine mammals were a prominent motif.

At the time Europeans discovered the coast, the design and construction of longhouses was the domain of master craftsmen. These respected individuals supervised all phases of construction. Teams of men felled the great cedars the master chose for the beams. Other groups prepared the sight and planked

▶
The forest is consuming a village site at Skedans, or Koona, on Louise Island in the Queen Charlottes. Trees 150 years old or more are using the longhouse timbers as nurse logs. — *Skedans, Queen Charlotte Islands, B.C.*

▶
Nearly 500 Haida of both the eagle and raven clans lived at Skedans. At its peak, the village consisted of 27 dwellings and featured 56 carved monuments. — *Skedans, Queen Charlotte Islands, B.C*

▶
Carved totems were used as longhouse frontal poles, inside houseposts, and as single mortuary, double mortuary and vertical memorials erected to commemorate the dead. Vertical mortuary poles usually had only one carved figure on the bottom and an uncarved shaft sectioned off in segments to represent the deceased's property and wealth. — *Skedans, Queen Charlotte Islands, B.C.*

136

▲
The great Haida canoes were carved from massive cedars. Test holes were dug into the trees to check for soundness and inner rot. Hundreds of these culturally modified trees are still growing in the forests cloaking the Queen Charlotte Islands — *Graham Island, Queen Charlotte Islands, B.C.*

the walls and roof. The standard currency for employment was blankets; each skill demanding its own blanket-fare.

As with all developed cultures with utilitarian needs met, art assumed its place. Prestigious longhouses were decorated with orcas, sea lions and sea eagles by artisans inspired by the infinite waters. Entrances were decorated with totems and classic Haida graphics with bold lines of white, red and black.

Though reclamation by the rain forest is unyielding, the skeletal remains of a few great houses can still be discovered from Vancouver Island north into southeast Alaska. In the Queen Charlotte Islands, where the Haida people live today, many of the ancient villages are protected and considered sacred.

Among the northern-most bands of the Tlingit, Haida and Kwakiutl, the arts rose to spectacular prominence. In the quiet recesses of the Queen Charlotte's

Anthony Island, decaying totems tell the tales of a great people alive with imagination and creativity. Owls, frogs, bears, ravens, sea mammals, eagles and the people themselves are all reflected in the magnificent totems.

Wandering through the toppled and tilting poles at Ninstints, the rain forest returns, embracing and reclaiming the

▲
Master carvers would search through the forest to find the best cedar from which to carve canoes. When the vessels were completed, slaves would carry and drag them through the dense forest to the closest body of water. Remnants of many of these efforts were mysteriously left behind. Their wooden skeletons have been returning to the earth for 100 years or more. — *Graham Island, Queen Charlotte Islands, B.C.*

great trees of cedar loaned out over a century earlier. Gaps in the crowns fill with jade and emerald mosses where arching eagles' beaks have fallen away. Gray-green lichens trace the seams and delicate cuts outlining grizzly faces and killer whale flukes. Around one totem base, the cubes of decaying cedar form a geometric puzzle created by time. For this pole, the end is a storm away. Eventually, the spirits which came to life in the totem's tale will return to the rich humus and nuture a future forest.

The rain forest was far more than a collection of needle-leafed trees and abundant salmon. Beneath their boughs, the verdant forest understory was a warehouse of edible goods and a sacred place to nourish the spirit and body. Native people knew of scores of edible plants growing within the forest, although they took advantage of relatively few of them on a regular basis. The Kwakiutl bands were familiar with nearly two dozen types of berries and nuts, though hazelnuts were their favorite. Roots, tubers and inner bark layers were all part of the native diet.

Collecting the rain forest riches was the obligation of women and younger children. On rare occasion, when favorite berries came into season, whole families and villages would journey afield. If too distant, temporary settlements were erected to base the collecting. Indian Heaven, nestled between Washington's Mount Adams and Mount St. Helen's still displays footprints of the Indian bands which gathered yearly to collect and prepare huckleberries, dye clothes, trade goods and compete in horse racing and other sports.

More than plant life filled the plates of the coastal people. Bear, elk, deer, beaver, fox and otter were all available to supplement their diet. Mammals, as well as many species of waterfowl, added variety to the dinner table. The protein these animals offered was only part of their value. Fur specimens were greatly

◄
Many stories about the figures on totems are only speculative. The true meanings were lost when the owners of the poles died. — *Skedans, Queen Charlotte Islands, B.C.*

◄
In time, all that will be left of the remaining totems and longhouse timbers in native villages along the Pacific coastal forest will be the new trees which began life on their decaying hulks. — *Skedans, Queen Charlotte Islands, B.C.*

prized as barter goods and raw material for making clothing and ceremonial garments.

Mountain goats, uncommon in most areas, were highly prized for their wool coats. Women would make collecting forays into the forest filling their cedar-bark baskets with their soft, creamy-white hair. The goat wool was woven into blankets and clothing. The exquisite weavings by the Salish and Bella Coola became revered articles of trade throughout the length of the Pacific Coast.

Totems tell the tale of the animals. Bear and beaver were represented on most of them. Characteristically, beavers were depicted holding or gnawing a stick. Like beaver, people are the only other creatures which enter the forest with a clear objective of altering it for their own benefit.

When the paddle-tailed rodent first assumed prominence in coastal folklore is uncertain but it occurred long ago. After the last glacial retreat twelve thousand years ago, beaver the size of today's bear chiseled their way through the wetlands. Perhaps these oversized rodents created a lasting impression in the minds of these people.

Numerous creatures on the totems illustrate the complexity of relationships between the people and the forest. At one time or another, nearly every animal within the ecosystem was brought to life in story, painting and carving.

The Pacific coastal people were the creators of a magnificent cultural heritage and left a legacy of harmonious life with the forest. Centuries of first-hand forest knowledge offer a blueprint for a lifestyle compatible with the coastal rain forests.

Today, small groups of remaining Indian bands are fighting for their survival and for the survival of their tribal lands. Without them, the only blueprints disclosing their efficient ways will be those held in the brindled trunks of aging cedar totems returning to the earth.

▲
Only a small fraction of the totem poles, masks, canoes, bentwood boxes, tools, shamans' rattles, blankets, cedar bark clothes and other items used by native people have been preserved in museums. This totem was taken from the village at Skedans in the Queen Charlotte Islands. —
Queen Charlotte Islands Museum

ENDANGERED SPACES

7he relationship between humans and the rain forest has taken a devastating turn in the last 150 years. The decreasing distance between need and greed has climaxed in a severe crisis which the forest and its inhabitants are struggling to survive.

Humans and the coastal forests of western North America existed in relative harmony for thousands of years. But as the riches of the forests became evident to pioneering lumbermen, entire groves of massive trees were cut with a fervor. This marked the beginning of the forests' demise.

At first, the forest seemed endless. Thousands of square miles covering two countries was more than anyone could see or comprehend. Few considered the course of history and took note of the fact that many forests all over the world were already extinct. Humans had stripped them, leaving the following generations to look elsewhere. Forests seemed an infinite resource. Ancient trees continued to fall victim to the saw. Abandoned stumps bleached in the sun and rendered what nutrients they could to new seedlings which sprouted in their vicinity. Nature abhors a vacuum, so young trees took root among the scattered remnants of giants, many of which had witnessed life on the coast since the time of Christ.

At first, the pace of cutting was slow enough to allow neighboring stands to replant the voids from their own stock. In light of nature's instincts to thrive, timbermen thought nothing was wrong; nature would seed new generations of timber. Their reasoning was flawed, and their faith in nature naive.

Since pioneers first encountered the deep-green carpet which covered the western edge of the continent, the onslaught of the forests has been relentless. Viewed as an endless resource, the wealth and prosperity it could bring to any company willing to lay chainsaw to timber was an incredible draw. California's gold rush in the mid-1800s signaled the beginning of of an insatiable demand for timber.

In the United States, the cutting on private land was so intense that by the 1930s, timber companies and the Forest Service finally began to realize what might happen when private holdings were depleted. By the mid-forties, private timber companies had consumed most of their holdings and yet virtually did nothing to replace them.

The more valuable ancient forests disappeared quickly — one acre of ancient forest yields ten times as much as second growth. Large, private companies turned to federal lands. During the years of their own prosperity, they discouraged the cutting of federal land to keep prices up. But with the Second World War, the rush of progress slammed right into the great conifer woodlands of the coast.

The hard-hit private companies and the government agencies created to assure the care and survival of the forest harvested them mercilessly in order to supply the military and the families who produced the post-war baby boom. Even before the war ended, professional foresters warned the agency that its commitment to sustainable yield (protecting the

◄
A thin line of trees left along the water's edge is not enough to protect lakes, rivers and streams. Between stream damage caused by forestry practices and overfishing by such methods as driftnetting in the open ocean, the world's most productive salmon runs have been reduced to a fraction of their former abundance.
— Prince of Wales Island, Alaska

**Chapter title page —
Clearcutting on native corporation-owned land —**
Prince of Wales Island, Alaska

▲
Vast expanses of the ancient rain forest have been removed for the economically valuable timber. The cutting has been so intense for so long that the ecosystem and its inhabitants — both plants and animals — are in serious danger. Modern forest management reduces biological diversity by destroying and fragmenting habitat, and by creating sterile tree farms in which few highly-adapted ancient forest plants and animals can exist. — *Nimpkish Valley, Vancouver Island, B.C.*

forest so it would continue to provide its valuable services forever) would not be met, particularly because funds for reforestation were insufficient.

Still, no one slowed the pace. As private timber companies demanded more, the cut in the national forests had increased 400 percent by the mid-sixties.

The clearcutting continued unabated until the 1970s. In the mid-seventies, Congress ordered the Forest Service to adhere to its original mission of limiting the cut to only what the forests could withstand in perpetuity. Overcutting, removing trees faster than new ones could grow back, was to be curtailed.

By adopting the National Forest Management Act (NFMA) of 1976, each of the 156 national forests was to write a ten-year plan that would detail harvesting and other forest uses, such as recreation, watershed protection and wildlife habitat protection and restoration. From studies conducted to formulate these

Clearcutting removes all trees — even young ones which cannot be used for lumber — but not all the wood is used. Like this cedar dropped in a city dump in British Columbia, much is burned, left to rot, used for firewood or simply wasted. — *Queen Charlotte Islands, B.C.*
▼

plans, forests managers conceded the harvests would have to decrease significantly. Some managers doubted even those reductions would be enough.

As plans neared completion seven years later, the Department of Agriculture, under which the Forest Service operates, pulled the plans during the Reagan administration. When it became evident that timber harvests in each of the national forests along the West Coast would be lowered, they order a review. At the same time, Congress ordered the agency to increase sales, although the overcutting violated Forest Service mandates. Eight years later, the plans were still not in effect.

By the 1980s, what little ancient forest was left on private land was owned by small companies which had been harvesting at a sustainable rate. But they were being watched by large corporations. Some bought out the small firms in Wall Street raids. They cleared the trees and sold the wood overseas for a fast profit, mostly to the ravenous Japanese market, to pay off the debt with which they made the purchase.

Timber from federal lands is not to be sold overseas, but loopholes allowed a large amount to be sent to foreign markets. In one year, 25 percent of the unprocessed logs cut in Oregon and Washington were exported to Japan.

When timber companies were able to make greater profits elsewhere, mills closed and mill towns were boarded up. A public relations strategy promoted the mistaken belief that the battle to preserve ancient forests caused timber workers to lose their jobs. The slash-and-run rate of cutting grew to unprecedented levels. Private timber companies liquidated their stocks of ancient trees at a rate that devastated fish runs, further threatening already endangered wildlife. They scarred the landscape so badly that people from across the nation, including legislators, began to cry out for reform.

Ostensibly, the Forest Service is man-

◄
As forests around the world are diminishing and human population has increased to a staggering level, the demand for wood is higher than ever. Unprocessed logs, cut from the Pacific forest as well as tropical forests around the equator, are exported to one of the world's most wood-hungry nations, Japan, where a housing boom has pushed the demand. But Japan does not use all the unprocessed logs it purchases. Some are stored for later use, and perhaps, for resale. It is not unreasonable to think that the United States and Canada may one day import its own wood when the supply becomes seriously diminished. The export of raw logs is a factor in the rise in unemployment in the timber industry. — *Port of Astoria, Oregon*

◄
Thin, unstable soils are typical of the Pacific region. It is often difficult or impossible to replant steep hillsides. The trees which originally grew on such sites began life when a certain set of natural conditions allowed their colonization. Without those conditions, the land may never again support tree growth. — *Graham Island, Queen Charlotte Islands, B.C.*

dated by Congress to sell timber in order to make money for the federal government. But it is well documented that the Forest Service loses as much as $2 billion per year — a loss covered by taxpayers.

In 1990, the current year for which figures are available, it is estimated the Forest Service spent $370 million preparing for timber sales alone. Only twenty-three of the 155 forests in which logging is allowed made money. The twelve forests in the Pacific region, the most productive area in the country, made money. They generated $189 million and helped bring the total loss down to $175 million.

The nation's largest national forest, the seventeen-million-acre Tongass in southeast Alaska, loses the most money

of all the national forests. Its sad story is rooted in an idea with good intentions but whose implementation was wrong from the start.

In Alaska's early years, selling its natural resources was viewed as a way to encourage settlement and economic development. The Forest Service assisted this mission by helping entice large timber companies to move in. In their minds, smaller, locally-owned operations did little to boost the economy.

In the 1950s, two giant pulp mills took up residence in southeast Alaska — one owned by an American company, the other by the Japanese. The latter was seen as a way to boost Japan's post-war economy, especially since it had ceded its

▲
The Pacific forests holds more carbon contained in live and dead trees than any other terrestrial ecosystem in the world. When the forest is cut, large amounts of carbon are released into the atmosphere. Some of this carbon is released when wood, left over from clear-cutting operations, is burned in slash piles. Excess carbon in the atmosphere is a major component of ozone depletion and subsequent global warming. — *Six Rivers National Forest, California*

timber-producing lands to China and the Soviet Union. To get and keep them there, the Forest Service offered them a near-monopoly on the timber by awarding them fifty-year contracts at bargain-basement rates.

But even at prices as low as 3 percent of the value of the timber, the companies failed to keep enough Alaskans employed, let alone stabilize the economy. Conservationists were livid and fought for a change in the status quo.

In adopting the Alaska National Interest Lands Conservation Act in the 1980s, Congress set aside one-third of the Tongass as wilderness, with only about 9 percent of that being ancient forest. But Congress also dealt a blow by guaranteeing the timber companies an unusually-high cut, along with giving the Forest Service at least $40 million a year to prepare for timber sales and build miles of roads. The economy of southeast Alaska has still not improved.

In some years, the Forest Service lost as much as 93¢ on every dollar it spent preparing for timber sales in the Tongass, some of which never took place.

In 1990, the conservationists' fight to change such practices in the Tongass came to an end with the passage of the Tongass Timber Reform Act. Considered a compromise with which neither side was completely happy, the Act did set

Clearcutting is the most prevalent timber operation in the Pacific forest. Other cutting practices such as selective logging, thinning cuts and shelterwood cuts (those which leave enough trees to shade the ground) are not often used. In clearcutting, loggers leave enormous stretches of land exposed to rain, which causes soil erosion.
— *Siuslaw National Forest, Oregon*

▼

Ugly clearcut scars, mill closures, unemployment, losses in wildlife populations, erosion, and declining wild-salmon runs, pointed to a dying ecosystem and began to turn the tide against the old forestry practice of clearcutting. Conservationists rightfully contended that while trees were a renewable resource, ancient trees from 250 to two thousand years old were not. Nor were the ecosystems in which they grew.

Armed with proven scientific information gathered by professionals and with facts which they had gathered on their own, conservationists challenged the Forest Service using their own guidelines created to measure the health of the forest. Equipped with enough scientific data to stop the degradation, they halted timber sales and sued the Forest Service for wrecking havoc on the environment. They filed petitions with the U.S. Fish and Wildlife Service to list endangered animals citing the National Forest Management Act, the National Environmental Policy Act and the Endangered Species Act.

National attention was gained in 1987 when a petition to list the northern spotted owl as an endangered species was filed with the U.S. Fish and Wildlife Service. For the next three years, a battle raged to protect this little-known and little-seen animal and the habitat to which it is bound. The war over the woods began.

The timber industry sent up a cry they hoped would be heard in halls of Congress. They contended scores of jobs would be lost, mills would close and communities would be abandoned. But their campaign was flawed. Countless jobs had been lost already because of falling prices, automation in the mills and in the field, and through a fast increase in the export of logs to Japan.

Three years later, the spotted owl was listed as threatened throughout most of its range and an extensive battle to save it and the failing timber industry began.

Forests along the edges of clearcuts are left vulnerable to severe environmental conditions. Clearcuts are hotter, drier, colder, windier and accumulate more snow. Blowdowns from strong winds and exposure to extremes in climate often damage intact forests. — *Graham Island, Queen Charlotte Islands, B.C.*

Tree roots hold the soil. After clearcutting, these roots decompose before new trees can grow to bind the soil. Erosion then occurs on steep slopes and natural drainages. The resulting erosion washes soil down hillsides, clogging streams and destroying habitat for a variety of animals. — *Near Carmanah Valley, Vancouver Island, B.C.*

aside an additional million acres of ancient forest in wilderness areas. It also made major modifications in the fifty-year contract and repealed the automatic $40 million appropriation to the Forest Service. The mandated cut level was also lowered to one that approached sustainable yield.

For years, conservationists spoke out against the harvesting of ancient forests. Scores of foresters, biologists, hydrologists, mycologists, geologists and other professionals gathered enough evidence to prove that the forest and its inhabitants were suffering irreparable damage from clearcutting. And people began to listen.

►
With the Alaska Native Claims Settlement Act in 1971, 44 million acres of forest lands were given over to native Americans who formed regional and village corporations. The corporations have allowed the clearing of every single tree from some of these lands. In southeast Alaska, entire islands have been clearcut by native corporations. Some of these islands were used for decades by the ancestors of the corporation members. — *Prince of Wales Island, Alaska*

►
While clearcutting increases habitat and, therefore, populations of some species of animals (mostly those which are adaptable to a variety of habitats), it decreases biological diversity by removing habitat to which other species are inextricably tied. Deer and some species of birds flock to older clearcuts because of the availability of food — chiefly weedy, colonizing species. Other animals such as Vaux's swifts and spotted owls are diminishing in population because their homes are being destroyed. — *South Moresby, Queen Charlotte Islands, B.C.*

In British Columbia, most of Vancouver Island and 85 percent of the mainland is publicly-owned forest. Unlike federal forests in the United States where logging is regulated and logging rights are awarded in a competitive bidding process, the provincial government grants long-term tree farm licenses to timber companies to harvest and manage the land at no cost.

The Ministry of Forests does not oversee timber operations and has given the companies insufficient guidelines concerning the protection of other forest resources, such as fisheries, wildlife and historic sites. Additionally, the public is all but shut out of the process. Under the licenses, the timber companies set their own policies and logging and recreation plans. They are even allowed to ignore new scientific data and conduct their own research, though few of them employ hydrologists, fisheries biologists, wildlife managers or soil scientists.

It is estimated that the companies have wantonly deforested 92 percent of the ancient forest areas. Yet no one knows for certain, as the public is not allowed access to harvesting records, nor to the amount of money the government generates by the tree farm licenses.

The plundering of British Columbia's forests is worse than that of the United States. Clearcut areas extend up to 73 square miles. Loggers often cut steep slopes all the way down to major salmon streams. Roads are built so poorly that the soil bleeds down hillsides with the slightest bit of rain. The cutting is so intense that the goal of sustainable yield has been totally abandoned.

In Canada, conservationists have less legal recourse so drastic steps must be taken. They have formed alliances with native people who contend that because they never signed treaties ceding their tribal lands, the government does not have the right to award the lands to anyone else.

The battle to save the South Moresby

Wilderness on the Queen Charlotte Islands from clearcutting was finally won after fourteen years of relentless commitment by the Council of the Haida Nation, the Islands Protection Society and hundreds of concerned people. They refused to let an area which still bears the remains of the Haida people be logged, burned and planted in a monoculture tree farm.

Another powerful tool wielded in British Columbia is public opinion. By generating support from thousands of residents and taking their cause to the rest of the world, conservationists have begun the long battle to save what little remains of Canada's temperate rain forest.

The government can remove land from harvesting, but under the tree farm licenses (which the government awards gratis) there is a stipulation that the timber companies must be compensated for any amount over 5 percent withdrawn from logging. The province pays dearly to get its own land back. Over $30 million (Canadian) was promised when the South Moresby National Park and Reserve was created in 1986.

But monoculture plantations continue to be planted. It takes little imagination to recognize the differences between a mature coniferous rain forest and cloned tree farm.

The rain forest is an endless source of goods. The vitality of the system and its survival depends upon it. It is similar to a market where goods and services are constantly being exchanged, bartered, swapped, lost and on occasion, stolen. Every creature and each system attempts to garner the best possible deal for the price. In a monoculture tree farm, choices are limited to a sole commodity.

The ancient forest is a resource of inestimable value both economically and biologically. Unfortunately, its economic value has been its undoing. Biologically, the ancient forest of western North America benefits the world. The forest

Overleaf — The loss of the ancient rain forest also means the loss of many species. As the land is cut either in large swatches or small patches, habitat is lost. In patch cutting, habitat is fragmented and species decline both in number and in population. — Near Carmanah Valley, Vancouver Island, B.C.

protects the soil, cools the air, collects water, cleanses the atmosphere and replenishes oxygen.

As a major storehouse of carbon, forests help slow the pace of global warming. Carbon dioxide is sent into the atmosphere when plants decompose naturally or are burned and when fossil fuels such as gas, oil and coal, are burned. Through photosynthesis, plants absorb carbon dioxide and use it to grow.

As the levels of carbon dioxide released into the atmosphere in the last forty to fifty years increased, coniferous forests became vital purifiers. The needles on an ancient tree, assisted by a

▲
Tree farms are planted with a single species of tree, the seeds of which are taken from what foresters believe are the largest, strongest or fastest-growing trees. Monoculture plantations are vulnerable to widespread damage or total destruction because the trees' genetic makeup and their ability to fight disease and insect infestation is limited. — Gifford Pinchot National Forest, Washington

▲
Nature struggles to sur-
vive despite the slash-
and-burn harvesting of
ancient rain forests.
Bunchberry is a pioneering
species in cleared areas.

covering of fungi, absorb carbon dioxide and other air pollutants and transform them into useful nutrients. An ancient tree can contain as many as sixty million needles, making them quite adept at cleansing the air.

Additionally, the Pacific forest holds the greatest amount of biomass (leaves, needles, trunks, roots, soil, fallen trees and standing dead snags) of any forest in the world. As such, it is a significant carbon bank. When this bank is removed or altered, a massive amount of carbon is released into the atmosphere. Though young, fast-growing trees, such as those grown in plantations, absorb carbon quickly, they are small and have fewer needles. As a result, they are unable to absorb the tremendous amounts of car-

bon released as wood decays or is burned to clear the soil. In an old forest, the balance between decay and growth keeps the carbon cycle in check.

The ancient Pacific forest harbors the largest number of coniferous tree species of any forest in the world and each of these species is genetically diverse. The more diverse a species, the more adaptable it is to its physical setting and to changing conditions.

Genetic diversity is eliminated when forests are clearcut and the land subsequently planted in a monoculture. The monoculture seeds were chosen from what foresters believed were the tallest, strongest and fastest growing trees, however, none of these attributes ensured the viability of a tree. And they certainly do

▲

Second-growth tree plan-
tations have taken the
place of ancient forests on
much of the Pacific Coast.
While such plantations
produce lumber in forty to
eighty years, no one
knows how many rotations
the land will be able to
sustain for healthy tree
growth. Tree farms in
Europe and in eastern
North America have pro-
duced trees of poor quality
by their third rotation. —
Central Coast Range,
Oregon

The bark of the Pacific yew yields a useful cancer-fighting chemical. Yews grow as tall shrubs or small trees only in the shaded understory of ancient forests. Long considered a useless tree, until recently, the yew was thrown into slash piles and burned after ancient forests were clearcut.

▼

not ensure the viability of an entire plantation. Diversity gave the earth its rich variety of plants and animals and as we have seen, the loss of some species has made the earth poorer.

As a storehouse of genetic diversity, ancient forests hold secrets to life. Nearly 40 percent of the drugs Western doctors prescribe contain elements first found in nature. The Pacific forest harbors several of these drugs.

Digitalis, a heart stimulant used by cardiac patients, is derived from a local flower. The cascara tree contains a laxative. And taxol, a drug extracted from the bark of the Pacific yew, is used to treat cancer.

The Pacific yew is found only in ancient forests. It is an extremely slow-growing species. A hundred-year-old tree may only be four to five inches in diameter. A tree this size yields little bark. Cancer researchers have asked for 750,000 pounds of bark to conduct clinical tests, which foresters estimate will take up to forty thousand trees. With nearly 85 percent of the ancient forest gone, and much of the remainder scheduled for harvesting, researchers will have to work quickly to synthesize taxol in their laboratories. There are simply not enough yew trees.

The Pacific forest is also proficient at collecting and controlling water. The uncontrollable winter rains of the western coast of North America are not a problem for the ancient forest. The roots of old, living conifers brace the soil, helping to prevent erosion. The soil holds moisture for later use or sends it slowly into a multitude of streams and rivers.

Another service the ancient forest provides is ambient-water collection. By virtue of its multi-layered structure, the forest gleans moisture from the atmosphere by intercepting fog. Thirty percent of the water supply in the Douglas fir region is captured by the ancient forest canopy, a service most useful when water levels are drastically reduced during times of drought. With no trees to capture ambient moisture from passing clouds and fog, it passes by unused.

The forest also lessens flooding by intercepting heavy rains and snow. The giant limbs of ancient conifers intercept the rain and send it trickling instead of pouring onto the soil. In winter, they catch the snow, which then dissipates into the air or melts slowly to the ground. When spring rains hit the deep snow piled in clearcuts, the resulting rush of water sends soil downhill, cuts into stream banks destroying habitats for water animals and continues downstream, threatening towns and cities.

Fishing is a large industry in the

155

▲

Ancient forests increase water levels in city reservoirs by capturing moisture from fog and passing clouds, a service most useful during the typically dry summer months much of the Pacific forest experiences.
— *Swift Creek Reservoir, Gifford Pinchot National Forest, Washington*

waters off the Pacific forests. Thousands of people are supported by an industry whose wholesale value is $4 billion annually. But where the fields of ancient timber have suffered extensive logging and destruction, fish runs have been dramatically diminished.

When Lewis and Clark drifted down the Columbia River, sixteen million salmon and steelhead filled the waters of the Columbia Basin — a region spanning Oregon, Washington, Idaho, Montana and parts of Canada. The runs have dropped to as low as 2.5 million and of that number, only about three hundred thousand are wild fish. Nearly twenty-five native-salmon runs are extinct. Logging and a multitude of hydroelectric dams have taken a considerable toll, and the people who rely on the once-famous Pacific salmon for a living are suffering. Throughout the Pacific forest, the story is similar. Overcutting sent soil downhill, filling the streams and rivers, and

destroyed spawning grounds. Even hatcheries, built to raise the numbers of fish that were drastically reduced after construction of the dams, have not helped and have even proven harmful to native stock.

An intact forest also supplies a wealth of edibles. At least ten species of fungi are harvested from old forests. The best known, drawing top dollar for foragers and others supplementing their incomes, are chanterelle mushrooms and the underground Oregon white truffle, a fungi of exceptional flavor used in small quantities to flavor dishes. Other fungi, such as the cauliflower mushroom, oyster mushroom, angel wings and sulphur shelf fungus also grow under the canopy of trees formed only after ten or more decades of growth.

The forest yields other foods as well. Fiddlehead ferns carpet the forest floor, crawdads line streams and sweet berry bushes dot the landscape throughout the

▲
The ancient forests on
these small islands are
being reduced to small
patches in a quiltwork of
clearcuts and tree plantations. — *Near Prince of
Wales Island, Alaska*

Pacific forest. Though some of these gourmet foods don't necessarily require the ancient forest, they do require a healthy ecosystem.

Of all the products and services the ancient-forest ecosystem provides, the one most exploited is its close, straight-grained, knot-free, rot-resistant wood. The ancient, tall trees are ideal for a variety of purposes, though some of them are rather mundane.

The majority of conifer species growing in the Pacific forest are used for lumber (two-by-fours, beams, plywood and roof shingles) or for pulp (paper, cardboard, toilet paper and disposable diapers). These purposes seem wanton compared to others for which only ancient wood will do, such as high-quality musical instruments and fine furniture.

As the thousand-year-old trees are harvested to extinction, their value soars. Only when they are gone will we truly realize their worth. Once the ancient forest is cut, it will never return.

In terms of modern forestry, ancient forests are something corporate profits can not ignore. Foresters plan forty- to eighty-year rotations, but ancient forests are the product of eons of gradual growth and change.

The ancient forest is a priceless resource the world can not afford to lose. Yet we cling to the illusion that we can manage this diverse treasure.

Emotions run high on the issue. Some think of the forest merely as a wood crop intended for humans to harvest and use. Others see it as a an ecosystem, which left intact benefits all life by virtue of its resources.

But one thing is certain. A forest and a tree plantation are two entirely different things. How we choose to treat the few remaining tracts of America's rain forest is a decision with which the rest of the world will have to live — forever.

ACKNOWLEDGMENTS

In the rain forest, nothing is created in isolation. All things depend on predecessors. So, too, are the words and photographs contained in this book. In many ways they are the result of those who have walked the forests of the Pacific Coast before us, and like we, have fallen in love with their majesty and beauty. It is impossible for us to thank them all. We have drawn upon many for reference, knowledge, occasionally a meal and often friendship. To all, our kindest and warmest thanks. No matter how great or small, each bit of help was important. To the following people and organizations, a special thank you for contributing in helping *America's Rain Forest* become a reality:

Rick Brown, National Wildlife Federation; Jean Cross; Bill Dennison; Michael Durham; Paul Englemeyer and Mary Sculley, Ten Mile Creek Association; Leonard Feldis, Ministry of Forests, Canada; Bob Freimark, The Wilderness Society; Joe Foy and Mark Wareing, Western Canada Wilderness Committee; Lou Gold and Beth Howell, Siskiyou Regional Education Project; Ian Gray, Partridge Television and Video Ltd.; Stanley Held; Charis Henrie; Carol and Warren Krager; Marc Liverman, Portland Audubon Society; Natalie McFarland, Queen Charlotte Islands Museum; Jerry Meirs Bureau of Land Management; Andrew Moldenke, Oregon State University, Department of Entomology; Ernie Meloche; Paul McIntosh, Tom DeMeo and Paul Brewster, Tongass National Forest; Kim Nelson, Oregon State University, Department of Fisheries and Wildlife, Frank Oliver, Bureau of Land Management; Randal O'Toole; Bret Sellers; Christopher Skagen; Skidegate Band Council; Southeast Alaska Conservation Council; Squeek & Weezle; Stephen Suddes, Canadian Park Service; Dan Taylor, National Audubon Society; Dave Ward, Oregon Department of Fish and Wildlife; Barbara Wilson; and Matt Zaffino.

A special thanks to Matt "Big Guy" Phillips who endured my cooking, strange sense of humor and rainy nights in the back of the Sube to help make the photography and the forest more than memories on film.

AUTHOR'S NOTE

This book is Gerry's. It was borne of a creative mind and a fierce commitment to saving all components of our natural world, particularly the temperate rain forest. His tireless efforts to create this book gave me the opportunity to inspire others to do the same. So, to my husband, heartfelt gratitude and thanks for the chance to work alongside you on a project that I, too, felt was important. Thanks also to my co-workers at the Washington Park Zoo who put up with my temporary insanity as I worked on projects that I hope will make a difference in the world.

Special thanks to my editor, John Ferguson, for his praise and encouragement, and especially to the publishers, Tom and Pat Klein, for embracing the idea and giving us a forum to share our love and knowledge of the ancient forest.

PHOTOGRAPHER'S NOTE

There were great highs and lows to photographing the images that spill across these pages. Sadly, some of the scenes that were recorded on film have been lost for eternity to the greed of the corporate chainsaw. In many places throughout the Pacific Coast the sky now touches the charred and barren ground where only two years ago, at this book's start, it embraced the canopy three hundred feet aloft. The joy of watching spotted owls flirt before the camera and the pain of knowing owls that had been murdered out of stupidity and ignorance brought to a head the senselessness of the war being waged on the wilderness. I hope the beauty of the images in this book will thank those that have given so much and inspire others who did not know how much we have to lose.

SOURCES

BOOKS

Arno, Stephen F., and Ramona Hammerly. 1977. *Northwest trees*. Seattle: Mountaineers.

Bever, Dale N. 1981. *Northwest conifers*. Portland, Ore. Binford Mort.

Carey, Neil G. 1989. *Guide to the Queen Charlotte Islands: 1989-90 edition*. Anchorage, Alaska: Alaska Northwest.

Clark, Ella E. 1953. *Indian legends of the Pacific Northwest*. Berkeley, Calif.: Univ. of California Press.

Dorst, Adrian, and Cameron Young. 1990. *Clayoquot: On the wild side*. Vancouver: Western Canada Wilderness Committee.

Elkman, Leonard. 1962. *Scenic geology of the Pacific Northwest*. Portland, Ore: Binford Mort.

Ervin, Keith. 1989. *Fragile majesty: The battle for America's last great forest*. Seattle: Mountaineers.

Fitzhugh, William W., and Aron Crowell, eds. 1988. *Crossroads of continents: Cultures of Siberia and Alaska*. Washington, D.C.: Smithsonian.

Forsyth, Adrian, and Ken Miyata. 1984. *Tropical nature*. New York: Macmillan.

Gustafson, Paula. 1980. *Salish weaving*. Seattle: Univ. of Washington Press.

Hansen, Mel. 1977. *Indian heaven back country*. Beaverton, Ore.: Touchstone Oregon.

Hewes, Jeremy J. 1988. *Redwoods*. New York: Smith Pubs.

Kaysing, Bill. 1990. *Great hot springs of the west*. Santa Barbara, Calif.: Capra Pr.

Ketchum, Robert, and Carey D. Ketchum. 1987. *The Tongass: Alaska's vanishing rain Forest*. New York: Aperture

Kirk, Ruth, and Joshel Namkung. 1966. *The Olympic rain forest*. Seattle: Univ. of Washington Press.

Kelly, David. 1990. *Secrets of the old growth forest*. Layton, Utah: Gibbs Smith.

Kozloff, Eugene N. 1976. *Plants & animals of the Pacific Northwest*. Seattle: Univ. of Washington Press.

MacDonald, George. 1983. *Ninstints: Haida world heritage*. Vancouver: Univ. of British Columbia Press.

Maser, Chris. 1989. *Forest primeval: The natural history of an ancient forest*. San Francisco: Sierra.

Matthews, Daniel. 1988. *Cascade-Olympic natural history*. Portland, Ore.: Raven Edit.

Mitchell Beazley International, Ltd. 1981. *The international book of the forest*. Mitchell Beazley Publishers.

Mitchell, Andrew. 1986. *The enchanted canopy*. Great Britain: William Collins.

Muir, John. 1989. *The Yosemite*. San Francisco: Sierra.

Norse, Elliot. 1990. *Ancient forests of the Pacific Northwest*. Covelo, Calif.: Island CA.

O'Toole, Randal. 1988. *Reforming the forest service*.Covelo, Calif.: Island CA.

Perlin, John. 1989. *A forest journey: The role of wood in the development of civilization*. New York: Norton.

Pyle, Robert M. 1986. *Wintergreen: Listening to the land's heart*. Boston: HM.

Ramsey, Jarold, ed. 1977. *Coyote was going there: Indian literature of the oregon country*. Seattle: Univ. of Washington Press.

Reid, Walter V. and Kenton Miller. 1989. *Keeping options alive: The scientific basis for conserving biodiversity*. Washington, D.C.: World Resources Inst.

Stewart, Hillary. 1984. *Cedar: Tree of life to the northwest coast indians*. Seattle: Univ. of Washington Press. 1990. *Totem poles*. Seattle: Univ. of Washington Press.

Stoltman, Randy. 1987. *Hiking guide to the big trees of southwestern British Columbia*. Vancouver: Western Canada Wilderness Committee.

Wallace, David R. 1983. *The Klamath knot*. San Francisco: Sierra.

Whitney, Stephen. 1989. *The Pacific Northwest: A Sierra Club naturalist's guide to the Pacific Northwest*. San Francisco: Sierra. 1985. *Western forests*. New York: Knopf

Wilcox, Lisa,. ed. 1989. *The rainforests: A celebration*. New York: Routledge Chapman & Hall. (Barrie & Jenkins UK).

Zucker, Seth. 1991. *Saving our ancient forest*. Los Angeles: Living Planet Press.

REPORTS

Franklin, Jerry, and C.T. Dryness. 1988. *Natural vegetation of Oregon and Washington*. Corvallis, Ore.: Oregon State Univ. Press. et al. 1981. *Ecological characteristics of old growth Douglas fir forests*. Portland, Oregon: U. S. Department of Agriculture, Pacific Northwest Forest and Range Experiment Station.

Maser, Chris and Bruce Mate. 1981. *Natural history of Oregon coast mammals*. Portland, Ore.: U. S. Department of Agriculture, Pacific Northwest Forest and Range Experiment Station. and James Trappe. 1984. *The seen and unseen world of the fallen tree*. Portland, Ore.: U. S. Department of Agriculture, Pacific Northwest Forest and Range Experiment Station.

Morrison, Peter, et. al. 1990. *Ancient forests in the Pacific Northwest: Analysis and maps of twelve national forests*. Washington, D.C.: The Wilderness Society.

Omernik, James M. 1986. *Ecoregions of the Pacific Northwest*. Corvallis, Ore.: U. S. Environmental Protection Agency, Environmental Research Laboratory.

Voegtlin, D. J. 1982. *Invertebrates of the H. J. Andrews experimental forest*. Corvallis, Ore.: Oregon State Univ. Press.

Wilderness Society eds. 1986. *America's vanishing rain forest: A report on federal timber management in southeast Alaska*. Washington, D.C.: The Wilderness Society.

The following magazines have published articles on the ancient forest.

Audubon Magazine, Nov. 1987; Nov. 1989; January 1990

Beautiful British Columbia Magazine; Winter 1989

Buzzworm, Jan/Feb 1990

Defenders of Wildlife, Sept/Oct 1990

International Wildlife, March/April 1991

Natural History, February 1985; August 1988

National Geographic, September 1990

The New Yorker, May 14, 1990

The Oregonian (Portland) special reports of October 15, 1990, November 29, 1990 and December 16, 1990

Orion Nature Quarterly, Winter 1990

Outside, December 1988

Register-Guard (Eugene, Oregon) special report of December 2, 1990

Sierra Magazine, July/August 1987; May/June 1991

Time, June 25, 1990

Wilderness, Spring 1988

World Magazine, Sept. 1990